THE EARTHIST CHALLENGE TO ECONOMISM

The Earthist Challenge to Economism

A Theological Critique of the World Bank

John B. Cobb, Jr.
Emeritus Professor
Claremont School of Theology, Claremont Graduate School
California

First published in Great Britain 1999 by
MACMILLAN PRESS LTD
Houndmills, Basingstoke, Hampshire RG21 6XS and London
Companies and representatives throughout the world

A catalogue record for this book is available from the British Library.

ISBN 0–333–73088–7

 First published in the United States of America 1999 by
ST. MARTIN'S PRESS, INC.,
Scholarly and Reference Division,
175 Fifth Avenue, New York, N.Y. 10010

ISBN 0–312–21838–9

Library of Congress Cataloging-in-Publication Data
Cobb, John B.
The earthist challenge to economism : a theological critique of
the World Bank / John B. Cobb, Jr.
p.   cm.
Includes bibliographical references and index.
ISBN 0–312–21838–9 (cloth)
1. World Bank.   2. Economics—Religious aspects—Christianity.
3. Economic man.   4. Sustainable development.   5. Environmental
degradation.   I. Title.
HG3881.5.W57C63   1998
332.1'532—dc21   98–28377
                                                                    CIP

This book is printed on paper suitable for recycling and made from fully managed and
sustained forest sources.

10   9   8   7   6   5   4   3   2   1
08   07   06   05   04   03   02   01   00   99

Printed and bound in Great Britain by
Antony Rowe Ltd, Chippenham, Wiltshire

Contents

Preface

For some years I have been moving from the critique of economic theory worked out with Herman Daly in *For the Common Good* to an effort to understand, as a Christian theologian, the major social changes and global events of recent years. I know that my knowledge of the details is woefully limited and that this can lead me into error. But I believe that theologians should not be intimidated by these inevitable limitations from addressing the issues that are of greatest importance to the future of humanity. Certainly we should do so humbly, and where I show my ignorance, I ask for help and correction. I hope the errors and omissions in detail do not invalidate the generalizations and perspectives that are the distinctive contribution of the theologian.

Some of my efforts to interpret recent world history were published in 1994 in *Sustaining the Common Good* (Pilgrim Press). Indeed, the schematism of Christianism, nationalism, economism, and Earthism that structures the present book appears briefly in one of its chapters. Except for 'nationalism' these terms are mine in the sense that when I first used them in the mid-eighties I was not aware of having heard or read them. The others are, of course, intended to parallel 'nationalism,' which I take to have been the publicly dominant religion of the modern period.

Later I discovered that 'economism' had been used by Joel J. Kassiola in 1990 in *The Death of Industrial Civilization* (SUNY Press). So far as he knows, he coined it, although neither of us would be surprised to discover earlier uses of this term. Our meanings are quite similar. In more recent years I have seen the noun, as well as the adjective 'economistic,' quite often. I hope more people will find this language useful in describing the religion of our time. The other terms may also have been used by others. Certainly in French 'Christianisme' is common, although not with just the meaning I have given it.

During my study I became increasingly aware of the important role of the Bretton Woods institutions – the International Monetary Fund and the World Bank – and felt impelled to understand them better. In studying them I was motivated at first by distress over what seemed to me their destructive actions, and I was tempted to attribute maliciousness or ignorance to their leaders. Because so many of their actions devastated the natural world and supported the interests of the rich and powerful against the poor and weak, I suspected them of callous indifference to nature and hypocrisy in their profession of concern for the poor. I suspected that they intended the results that, from my perspective, their policies in fact engendered.

But I gradually came to appreciate the depth of idealism, commitment, and intelligence they embodied. I realized that my disagreements were fundamentally religious or ideological, that it was the difference in fundamental perception or basic faith that led to my disapproval of some of their actions. I came to see the World Bank as the finest institutional expression of the economistic faith, remarkably effective in implementing its teachings, but also remarkably open to Earthist critiques. I began to wonder whether a conversion might be possible, so that the genuine intention to serve the poor and protect the environment could be channelled into environmentally responsible empowerment of the poor.

Aware that my account of the International Monetary Fund and the World Bank was based on limited and one-sided accounts, I shared earlier drafts of this manuscript with persons in better position to know. I am grateful for the critical support of Herman Daly and Robert Goodland. I also sent a copy to Lynn Sherburn-Benz. She sent me quantities of Bank publications and shared the draft with others at the Bank, who also gave me valuable criticisms.

Even more important, she arranged an invitation for me to spend a week at the Bank in August 1997, specifically in the Environment Department. I owe a great deal to Tim Cullen who issued the invitation and to Andrew Steer who was my host. Steer arranged for me to visit a dozen persons in the Bank and the International Finance Corporation, including Cullen and Steer, who were in position to answer many of my questions and to provide me with additional material. All were generous with their time and gracious in their attitude. My appreciation for the spirit of those who work at the Bank and my hope for its future leadership were enhanced by the visit. I have revised the manuscript considerably in light of what I learned.

One thing I learned is how ignorant I am, how much more there is to learn! In my revision I have tried to make clearer the very specific and limited task I am undertaking in the discussion of the Bank, that is, to trace the history of its self-understanding. Much of great interest about its history and current developments falls outside that purpose.

The book as a whole is a quite new undertaking. However, some of the material in Chapters 1, 2, and 10 was given at a 'Conference on New Paradigms for Old Earth: Speaking Across Cultures in a Global Ecosystem', held May 4–7, 1995, in Missoula, Montana. It was the third conference in a series, 'In the Thoreau Tradition.' The conference as a whole was an unusually rich experience, and I would particularly like to thank Annick Smith for organizing it and for including me.

A number of other people helped me at different points. They include David Griffin, Fred Register, and Benton Rhoades. I need hardly ask that I alone am held responsible for remaining errors in fact and judgment.

List of Abbreviations

BWI	Bretton Woods institutions
GATT	General Agreement on Tariffs and Trade
GDP	Gross Domestic Product
GEF	Global Environmental Facility
GNP	Gross National Product
IBRD	International Bank for Research and Development
ICSID	International Center for Settlement of Investment Disputes
IDA	International Development Agency
IFC	International Finance Corporation
IMF	International Monetary Fund
ISF	International Stabilization Fund
MAI	Multilateral Agreement on Investments
MIGA	Multilateral Investment Guarantee Agency
NAFTA	North American Free Trade Agreement
NGO(s)	Nongovernmental organization(s)
OECD	Organization for Economic Cooperation and Development
OED	Operations Evaluation Department
OPEC	Organization of Petroleum Exporting Countries
SAP(s)	Structural adjustment program(s)
TNC(s)	Transnational corporation(s)
UN	United Nations
WCC	World Council of Churches
WDR	World Development Report
WTO	World Trade Organization

Introduction

Economic goals dominate society all over the globe, and economic thinking determines how they are pursued. We have come to suppose that this is simply the rational, natural way to be. Many assume that when we free ourselves from all ideology we adopt this position of necessity. But this is wrong. Allowing economics to dominate society implies an ideology that on examination is quite strange and that has been accepted only quite recently.

From a humanistic point of view, the dominance of economic considerations is a reversal of traditional values, even those of the Enlightenment. From a naturalistic point of view, it neglects the worth of nature and leads to its destruction. From a communitarian point of view, it denies the profoundly social nature of human beings. From a democratic point of view, it involves the loss of popular sovereignty. From a Christian point of view, it is the idolatrous worship of mammon.

In our public life none of these objections are taken seriously. These points of view are all tolerated, but they are relativized. They are considered ideological, whereas the pursuit of economic growth is thought to be purely practical or pragmatic. The one goal that unifies the body politic is that of sustained economic growth. Economists are assumed to be those best qualified to guide us in this growth. The rest is secondary.

This culture is 'economistic,' and the spirit and ideology that move it constitute 'economism.' Economism functions today as our shared religion. The world it is producing is increasingly disturbing. Individuals in an economistic society are not expected to devote much attention to economism. Few of them study its basic principles. This is left to the experts. Instead, they devote themselves to competition in what is negatively described as the 'rat race.' This is done in order to acquire the wherewithal to purchase the goods and services that are understood to make life worthwhile. The popular embodiment of economism is consumerism.

If economism is the dominant religion of our time, it is worthy of closer examination. How did it come into being and then gain the adherence of the whole world? What is its theology?

1

What are the institutions through which it acts? How is it reshaping our society and the world? What are its positive contributions? What are its weaknesses and limitations? How long will it endure? What may succeed it? How may the next transition occur? These are the questions with which this book deals.

Chapter 1 reviews the history of the West in terms of the successive 'isms' or religions that have grasped and shaped it.

Chapter 2 singles out economism for further attention and describes the Earthism that is rising to challenge it.

Chapter 3 shows how more and more of society now functions for the sake of the market, that is, in the service of economism. This is true both in the United States and globally.

Chapter 4 describes the Bretton Woods conference as the initiation of the economistic age and the early history of the institutions established by it: the International Monetary Fund (IMF) and the World Bank.

Chapter 5 examines the changes that took place in the Bank under Robert McNamara, and the rise of global economic crisis brought about by the growing debt of Third World countries.

Chapter 6 describes structural adjustment programs (SAPs) as both a response to the debt crisis and a consistent application of the increasingly dominant neo-liberal ideology.

Chapter 7 traces the rise of opposition to the Bretton Woods institutions and describes the emergence of a coherent ideology that unites it.

Chapter 8 examines the paradigm out of which the Bank has come to operate as it attends to the criticisms it hears and undertakes to improve its programs for the poor and for the environment.

Chapter 9 describes changes occurring in the Bank in the nineties and especially in the Wolfensohn administration. It considers the possibility that the Bank might evolve into an Earthist institution.

Chapter 10 takes up the Earthist story that now challenges the economistic one, proposing to structure it in such a way as to express Christian convictions, and it concludes by making explicit the Christian Earthism of the author.

This book belongs to a genre that can be called 'ideology critique.' It includes extensive criticism of the policies and practices of the Bretton Woods institutions as these follow from and express the ideology that shapes them. There is no questioning of the sincerity and dedication of those who shape these policies and practices. But respect for those who have given themselves to the work of the IMF and the World Bank does not change judgments as to the actual effects of many of their efforts. Some of those effects appear, when viewed from a different ideology, the Christian Earthist one, to be devastating.

The production of evil by persons with pure hearts is nothing new. In the age of Christianism, saints persecuted Jews and led Crusades in order to overcome the enemies of their faith. One can recognize their sanctity and still disagree with their theology and be distressed by its results.

In the nationalist era, the nationalist saints (more often called heroes or patriots) led in imperial conquest, in mercantile competition, and above all in international war. They transformed the face of the Earth into a system of European Empires, generously bestowing the fruits of their national cultures upon the 'natives' they conquered and colonized. Those who resisted were slaughtered. Treason, the unpardonable sin, they punished by death.

The saints of the economistic age are the selfless experts and technocrats who devote their lives to the economic advancement of others, especially the poor. They, also, are inflicting horrors on the world out of their sanctity and professionalism. They are further disempowering and impoverishing the poor out of their conviction that only so can they save them from their poverty.

The lesson we are slow to learn is that, in world-historical terms, basic faith and ideology are more important than personal virtue. Unselfish devotion to what one believes to be good does not protect one from doing harm to others. Indeed, it may be that the world has suffered more from the devotion of its saints than from the viciousness of its criminals.

Unfortunately, it is difficult to persuade people today of the importance of ideology. The climate is anti-intellectual. What is important, most people think, is what we feel and do. Knowing what to do is not supposed to require asking any fundamental questions. Technical reason or pragmatic considerations are thought to suffice.

This attitude is encouraged by economism, which understands itself not to be an ideology at all, but purely a science, a rational mode of thinking with self-evident assumptions. The mind needs to be used, not for the examination of such assumptions, but only for deriving their consequences. It is for this reason that technical reason suffices.

The indifference to ideology flourishes also because the beliefs people think about and relativize are rarely the ones that actually shape their lives and their societies. They are more likely to be the ones that shaped past societies. Thus moderns find the differences in belief systems among various Christian denominations or between Christians and adherents of other 'world religions' curious, and even interesting, but quaint rather than important. Their concern is not to sort out the differences and make intellectually difficult judgments about them. Their concern is instead that adherents of all these traditional faiths live and work together peaceably today.

Hegel's famous phrase rings true. 'The owl of Minerva flies only in the evening.' It seems that we can reflect about ideas or beliefs only after they have ceased to shape us and world-historical events. Perhaps this applies to this book and its discussion of economism as well. Perhaps it is only because economism has already achieved its goal of reshaping the world that we can now objectify it and criticize it. Perhaps it is too late for such objectification and criticism to have any effect on the course of events.

Nevertheless, understanding where we are in the course of the history that sweeps us along can make a difference. Critical reflection will not bring an end to the reign of economism, but that reign will in any case come to an end eventually. Understanding it, and understanding alternatives to it, *may* contribute to a less destructive transition from its hegemony to that of another faith. That hope motivates the writing of this book.

In viewing both past and present, it is important to distinguish between Christians and Christianists. Christians place their faith in God as they know God in Jesus Christ. Christianists give themselves to the triumph of Christianity over other beliefs and communities. Many Christianists are such because of their belief that this is required by their faith in God as they know God in Jesus Christ. Some theological formulations of

Christian faith justify this conclusion. But Christian theology can also be so formulated as to warn against this deduction as idolatrous. Not all Christians are Christianists.

It is also important to distinguish between patriotism and nationalism. Again the transition from love of country and willingness to make personal sacrifices for its sake to 'my country right or wrong' is an easy one. Many explanations of what is involved in patriotism lead directly to nationalism. Patriots who criticize their nation because its actions are unjust to other peoples are often viewed as traitors. Nevertheless, there is a real difference, and it is possible to explain love of nation in such a way as to justify such criticism. One may even understand that refusal to serve in the armed forces can be an expression of patriotism. Not all patriots are nationalists.

The same distinction is needed today between economists and economistic thinkers. Once again the transition from socialization into the dominant forms of economic thought and commitment to economism is an easy one. Current economic orthodoxy includes teachings about nature, about human beings, and about world-historical processes that, when taken at face value, lead directly to economism. But it is also possible to understand these doctrines as abstractions useful for the analysis of the market, but not to be taken as final truths about reality. It is possible to affirm economic theory as extrenely useful in the understanding of a very important aspect of society, while recognizing that it describes only this one aspect of a society which rightly holds to other values as equally important with economic ones. In short, it is quite possible to be an economist without subscribing to economism. And it is certainly possible, and very common, to subscribe to economism without being an economist.

Economism is the belief that society should be organized for the sake of economic growth. Those who hold this belief assume that economic growth is good for human beings; so they do not hold to growth for growth's sake but for the sake of the well-being of human beings. Nevertheless, at least in the public world, they subordinate other ways of seeking the well-being of human beings to the economic one. In particular they subordinate national interests as understood in the period of nationalism to economic ends.

Commitment to economism encourages people to think that economic growth will quite directly solve a wide range of problems. Among the claims that thoroughgoing economistic thinkers have made for economic growth are that it will do away with poverty, end class conflict, stop population growth, lead to protecting the environment, generate full employment, and provide the resources for pursuing many other values. Not all economistic thinkers make such extensive claims, but in its purest form economism discourages the direct pursuit of other ends – environmental protection, for example – if such efforts slow economic growth.

Economistic thinkers may disagree as to how best to pursue growth. Nevertheless, with the demise of Communism and the decline of socialist thinking generally, a single closely related family of economic theories now constitutes the overwhelmingly dominant ideology of the economistic faith. 'Neo-liberalism' is a label that points to that family or at least to its currently dominant forms. In parts of this book neo-liberal doctrines are presented as *the* ideology of economism itself. This is an exaggeration, but one that does not seriously distort the current reality.

Adherence to economism is a matter of degree. An individual or a society may be more or less economistic. American society today has gone a long way in this direction. As a member of that society I have tendencies of this sort, although I resist them. As a Christian, I also have tendencies to Christianism, of which I am ashamed. And in certain contexts I also discover tendencies to nationalism, which I also regret.

Not all Christians have been ashamed of Christianist tendencies, not all Americans have opposed American nationalism, and not all who are caught up in contemporary economistic culture resist being economistic. In the purest cases of Christianism, Christianists defend devoting themselves to the advancement of Christianity as the one, most perfect, way of serving God. In the purest cases of American nationalsim, Americans see a global mission of the United States to extend American values around the world and to police it so as to ensure that opposing forces do not prevail. In the purest cases of economism, its supporters defend subordinating all the structures of society to the service of economic growth as the one, most perfect, way of serving humanity.

A Christian believer need not be a Christianist. But even those who agree with this may question whether a Christian can be an Earthist. Certainly, most have not been and are not now. One purpose of this book is to encourage more Christians to take this step.

An objection is that Earthism is idolatrous. Taken at face value, this is suggested by the term. A Christian cannot give supreme devotion to a creature, and the Earth is certainly part of creation.

It is striking, however, that many of those Christians who warn against Earthism on this valid basis seem oblivious to the more dangerous idolatries of Christianism, nationalism, and economism. A major contribution of Christianity to this type of discussion should be its sensitivity to the danger of idolatry, to treating what is creaturely as if it were God. But when this is done selectively against Earthism, by persons who support the dominant economism, it is itself more likely to be an expression of idolatry than of true faith.

Christians cannot, and should not, avoid giving penultimate loyalty to what at any given time in history offers promise of serving God through serving God's creatures. It has not been wrong to serve the church and the cause of Christianity with deep devotion. But it is wrong to do so when one forgets that the church and Christianity as a whole are not God and that they come under the judgment of God. When serving the church turns into making life miserable for those who reject it, or who understand Christianity in a different way, this difference has been forgotten.

Similarly, it is right for Christians to love their people and their nation. It is right to feel a deep kinship for those with whom one shares a common history, a common language, a common culture. It is right to serve them sacrificially. But when such service turns into the subjugation and destruction of other peoples, into failure to appreciate the equal justification of their love and service of their nations, then it has crossed the line into idolatry.

Again, it is right for Christians to care deeply for the economic well-being of all people. The economic well-being of people is not to be depreciated in terms of the greater importance of 'spiritual' values. Indeed, no act is more 'spiritual' than providing drinking water to the thirsty. To give oneself with great devotion to making more goods and services available as widely as possible is admirable. But when this commitment to achieving economic prosperity subordinates all other values to itself, when it claims that it is the solution, or the prerequisite to the solution, to all other important human problems, then it, too, has crossed the line into idolatry.

Christians should serve the church, their nations, and the production of goods and services. But treating any of these today as the penultimate commitment turns out to be inadequate and damaging. Today we need a more inclusive object of penultimate devotion.

The penultimate object of devotion suggested most readily by Christian faith is creation. Regrettably, for several centuries we Protestants have subordinated the traditional doctrine of creation to a focus on the relation of God and human history. Protestants are now repenting of that narrowing of our heritage. We came close to adopting humanism as an idolatry to replace faith in God, the Creator of *all* things. The World Council of Churches expressed our repentance of this error by reaffirming the integrity of creation as a central focus of concern. A large literature has appeared in all branches of Christianity dealing with the importance of the whole of creation.[1]

There remains a great gap between what is increasingly acknowledged and affirmed in leadership circles and the ordinary worship and practice of local congregations. But this is more a matter of cultural lag than of willful resistance. Few Christians now deny altogether that God cares for the whole of creation and that we should do so too. Some lead the way in such movements as 'creation spirituality.'

This suggests that Christians should advocate 'creationism' as the new religion and spirituality. This is certainly not wrong. But it has two limitations.

First, if we are to play any effective role in redirecting society away from the catastrophes toward which economism is leading it, we need to work together with others. 'Creationism' is too narrowly Christian to work well in this way. It is better to use a term that unites us with already existing movements in the wider society. A focus on the Earth serves well in this respect.

Second, even for Christians the whole of creation, meaning the universe with all its gallaxies, is not a practical or fruitful object of devotion. Perhaps some day the situation will change, but for the foreseeable future the part of creation which needs and deserves penultimate devotion is the Earth, inclusive of all its inhabitants and especially the human ones. Earthism directs our energies most appropriately.

Furthermore, to call for devotion to the Earth among Christians is continuous with much that is happening. The Earth is clearly the center of the creation story. Already many churches celebrate Earth Day. There are Christian magazines called 'Earth Spirit,' 'Spiritearth,' 'Earth Letter,' 'Earth Light,' and 'Earthkeeping News.' Christians make extensive contributions to another called 'Earth Ethics.' Concern for creation expresses itself overwhelmingly as concern for the Earth. To speak of Christian Earthism or Earthist Christianity is merely to name much that is already happening. Perhaps this book can further this movement as well.

NOTES

1. See my already outdated bibliography in the revised edition of John B. Cobb, Jr., *Is It Too Late? A Theology of Ecology*. Denton, TX: Environmental Ethics, 1995.

1 Christianism, Nationalism, and Economism

I. OUR HISTORIES

It is good to take stock at the end of a century. This time, the end of the century is also the end of a millennium; so the desirability of taking stock is heightened. At the close of the first millennium of the Christian Era, many expected the end of the world through supernatural apocalypse. There will be some of that expectation again this time. But more of us are concerned about another kind of apocalypse – one brought about by human pressure on planetary systems. In view of the real dangers that our century bequeaths to the next millennium, it behooves us all the more to try to understand who we are.

In the West the question of who we are is largely identified with where we are – where we are, that is, not so much spatially as temporally. What is our past, and what changes are now occurring? We all live, consciously or unconsciously, out of some sense of our place in the larger movement of history.

The historical account on which I was nurtured began in the fourth millennium BCE. In that story, what happened before then was prehistory, and what came before history really did not count. It was supposed that until people gathered in cities, organized societies, left written records, and constructed buildings that could be uncovered by archeologists, there was no civlization. And without civilization, human beings were viewed as 'savages,' and savages were hardly human. No one said that, but that was the implication. And it was an implication that had been internalized by Western peoples and had shaped their behavior.

In this account, history began in Mesopotamia and Egypt and had its first culmination in Greece; and any subsequent civilization that did not incorporate the achievements of Greece was, at best, exotic. The supposedly *real* course of human events from then on was restricted to those who carried on the legacy of Greece. This means, at first, essentially, the Roman Empire.

The Roman Empire split East and West. Its continuity was far clearer for a thousand years in the East. Nevertheless, the history I learned indicated that what happened there was not real history. Indeed, Eastern Europe was seen as ossified. The dynamic of history was lived out in the West through the collapse of the Roman Empire and the rise of the Holy Roman Empire. True history was the history of Western Europe. With the voyages of discovery and the vast movements of imperialism and colonization, the rest of the world was drawn into this history. The history of the West became global history, but still, it was assumed, the actors in that global history were Western Europeans.

There was a final shift in the eighteenth century. Prior to that time southern Europe was a full participant in history. But from then on real history was understood to be the history of northern Western Europeans and their colonies. Of these colonies, actually only those in North America counted. Instead of Western Europe, we thought of the North Atlantic countries as the bearers of history.

Today it is important to add that throughout this entire history males were the subjects or agents. Occasionally a woman exercised a male role, and this was recognized. But women who fulfilled women's roles in society were not participants in this history.

Those of the next generation may have been formed by a somewhat less narrow and self-serving view of human history. At the very least, some Asian countries, notably Japan, are recognized as now being agents in history. But it would be too much to say that the Eurocentric account outlined above has ceased to be formative in our educational system and in our culture. Much of the resistance to the cultural diversification of the university curriculum presupposes this understanding of where we are and, therefore, of who we are.

Of course, this view of history would not be so pervasive if it had no truth. When we seek to understand the forces that control the world today – politically, economically, and intellectually – we find that they have been formed primarily in the tradition described. Those who are committed to the continuation and further development of these forces naturally want to maintain the understanding of history with which they are connected.

Even those who are appalled by the destructive effects of these forces in the past and frightened by projections of their consequences into the future know that we must understand this history. Important as it is to learn the cultures and histories of all peoples, there is a special importance in learning how the forces now dominant in the world came to be the way they are. Approaching world history in this way, however, we will avoid the celebrative style in which it was typically written in the past. We will recognize that history has always been told from the perspective of victors, and that we should view what has happened and is happening also from the perspective of the victims.

We need to balance our study of how the dominant forces in today's world came to be the way they are with the study of other cultures and movements. There are several reasons for this. It provides us with a richer sense of the potentialities of humanness. It energizes and empowers persons who are not part of the dominant culture. It can give all of us a different sense of the history out of which we come and therefore a different view of who we are. It can also enable us to find in other cultures a wisdom that is lacking in the dominant one and ways to move into the future that do not simply project current trends. Today this openness of the Eurocentric reading of history to a role for other cultures is challenging the Eurocentrism itself, although it certainly has not overthrown it.

Still, to an impressive extent, the dominant culture is already being reshaped through its encounter with other cultures. This is clearest in the area of religious thought and sensibility. During the nineteenth century many supposed it would be only a matter of time before Western Christianity conquered the world religiously, as Western science and philosophy conquered it intellectually, and in fact Christianity did become a truly global faith. Nevertheless, the expectation that it would displace other great traditional ways has been falsified.

The most important effect of Christian missions in Asia was to revitalize ancient traditions there. In the twentieth century, missions generated by these revitalized traditions have been more effective in the West than continuing Western Christian missions have been in the East. Western Christianity is losing its convincing power even in the North Atlantic countries, or, more accurately, especially in them.

Within the longer world history I have summarized, there are many shorter ones dealing primarily with the 'West.' The standard one for the writing of history in my youth moved from the fall of the Roman Empire in the West to the Dark Ages. These were followed by the Middle Ages, the Renaissance, and the Enlightenment. Now many describe our situation as post-Enlightenment or 'postmodern' without yet being able to give this period a positive name. This history is written primarily in terms of considerations of culture and thought.

Another history is told from a socio-economic perspective. Feudal society was gradually displaced by the growth of cities and extensive systems of trade. The great transformation came with industrialization. Now we are living in the post-industrial age. This can be given a more positive label as the information age.

Less frequent, but perhaps equally important, is the religious or spiritual history of the West. Here 'religious' refers not just to what is traditionally called 'religion' but to whatever binds the multiple aspects of human existence together, and 'spiritual,' to supreme loyalty and devotion, that which gives meaning to life and identity to those who live it. The focus is not on the diversity of individual beliefs, but on the dominant force in society that shapes the options of its members. Viewed in this light, the second millennium CE can be surveyed in terms of three periods.

II. CHRISTIANISM

After the fall of the Western Empire, the major institution that survived was the Christian church. Its role was to provide a way of understanding the world that both shaped it and gave justification to other patterns that shaped themselves. The deepest explanation of phenomena – natural, cultural, social, political, and economic – was that provided by the church.

In later periods, partly in self-justification of the changed culture, the great age of Christianity was protrayed as superstitious, ignorant, and, in general, benighted. This is unfair. Medieval society was remarkably successful, even in economic terms. It was far from egalitarian, but it provided a meaning-ful place for most of its members. There was exploitation, but this was probably checked more than in earlier and sub-sequent periods. There were wars among feudal lords, but the church succeeded in imposing some limits on their destruct-iveness. Its artistic and intellectual achievements rank with the greatest the world has seen.

The church taught the ultimacy of God as object of devo-tion. This teaching can function to relativize the teacher. To whatever extent that actually happens, there is what Paul Tillich called a 'theonomous' culture. There was some authen-tic theonomy in the Medieval period.

Unfortunately, the primary emphasis was not on how devo-tion to God relativizes the claims of all creaturely institutions and communities. Instead, strong claims were made for the ability of the church to represent God on Earth and to speak for God. Belief in God tended more to absolutize the church than to relativize it. Human salvation was understood to depend on one's relation to the church, so that almost any action that established the relation approved by the church was regarded as justified.

Accordingly, I am calling the dominant religion and spir-ituality of this period, not theism, but 'Christianism.' For the sake of Christianity, hundreds of thousands of people took vows that deprived them of ordinary human enjoyments and freedom. Of course, other motives often entered in, including both faith in God and the desire for economic security. And in many individuals these other motives may have been domin-ant. But church and society were organized around the view that the fullest participation in Christianity required such sac-rifices, and society gave status to those who made them. It would be erroneous to minimize the genuineness of wide-spread devotion to the church.

For the sake of Christianity, hundreds of thousands of people, over several centuries, also marched off to recover the Holy Land from the 'infidel' Muslims. These believed in God just as strongly as did the Christians. They even gave a high place in their theology to Jesus, and they respected Christian-ity. But there was much in the teaching of the church that they rejected. And they certainly refused to accept the authority of the Roman pontiff. Out of devotion to Christianity Christians viewed the Muslims as unbelievers, and many Christians gave their lives to restore the Holy Land to Christian control.

Again, other motives were involved. For many, life at home was miserable or boring, and the Crusades gave a chance for respectable adventure. Some hoped to make a fortune through looting conquered cities. Nevertheless, if there had not been on the part of many a truly intense desire to recover the Holy Land from another religious group, there would have been no Crusades. The Crusades are evidence for the dominance of Christianism.

Christianity provided its own account of human history. This was set in the context of cosmic history. That is, it began with the story of creation. Since it affirmed that this creation was by a wholly good God, the evil in the world was explained by human rebellion against God. Because of God's goodness, God did not turn away from rebellious humanity, but instead continued working with and through selected persons and communities. In particular, God chose a community of despised slaves in Egypt, brought them out of that country and gave them the land of Palestine. God established a covenant with them, against which they often sinned. God sent prophets to warn them and finally sent 'His' own 'Son,' Jesus, who not only warned them but gave his life for their sake and for the sake of all people. God then raised Jesus from the dead. Those who believed in Jesus gathered in communities which God established as the church. This church administered the salvation effected by God in Jesus, so that those who believed would have eternal life while those who refused would be damned.

Not everyone in the West believed all the teachings of the church. Most emphatically, they were rejected by the Jews. But these believers in the God affirmed by the church suffered greatly for their resistance. Their role in society was import-ant, but their persecution testifies to the dominance of Chris-tianism.

Political leaders often resented the power of the church and worked to assert their own authority overagainst it. Since their military power greatly exceeded that of the church, one may ask why they were not more successful. The detailed answer is complex. But at its heart is the fact that they, too, lived and thought in the context of Christianism. Their arguments for greater autonomy from the church were usually couched in terms of Christian teaching. Few renounced the authority of the church altogether. Those few who did so could hardly be understood by their associates. Christianism was so taken for granted that political power could not be legitimated in other terms.

The real threats to the church were chiefly from those who believed it was not true to its own teaching. For centuries there were protests against the concentration of wealth in the church when its own sacred book affirmed the virtue of poverty. Some of these protests were channelled into movements within the church. Others became persecuted sects. Some of the protesters put their faith in God above their loyalty to the church. But none of these broke the dominance of Christianism.

These threats culminated in the Protestant Reformation. Many of the Reformers placed faith in God above their devotion to the church and even to Christianity as a system. The Reformation led to an intensification of personal devotion, and much of the Catholic response also expressed such intensification. Whereas previous protests against the Catholic Church had been contained or marginalized, this one shattered the basic unity of Western Christendom. But none of this led to the end of Christianism.

Indeed, the first half of the seventeenth century was the period in which Christianism became most intense. This intensity expressed itself in wars of appalling destructiveness. The Thirty Years War in central Europe is said to have reduced the population by one third. It was this orgy of mutual destruction that finally led to the decline of Christianism.

III. NATIONALISM

It was clear to many Christians that Christianity was no longer fulfilling the role of binding things together for society as a whole. It had, instead, become a principle of destructive divisions. There were good Christian reasons for seeking some other basis on which society could be ordered. The available candidates were the secular political leaders.

To call these leaders secular does not imply that they were not Christians. Indeed, it was these leaders who had led Catholic and Protestant forces into battle against one another. But a shift could be envisaged. Instead of understanding political leaders as in the service of Christianism, now embodied in competing forms, one could understand their primary role as establishing peace and order in their respective domains. This could be done either by establishing one or another form of Christianity and excluding others or by compelling the several forms of Christianity to tolerate one another.

The Treaty of Westphalia in 1648 symbolizes and embodies this shift. It expressed the willingness of persons who had previously considered the most important matter to be getting Christianity right to shift their priorities to civic order. This was to be maintained in a political unit – a city-state or a nation. Thus the nation, rather than the churches, became the ordering and unifying institution. The authority of the churches henceforth depended upon their being allowed to function by the state. This was the basic shift from Christianism to nationalism.

Few then, and fewer still today, would dispute the wisdom of this shift as a response to the fratricidal wars of that time. Surely the differences between Catholics and Protestants and Anabaptists do not justify mutual slaughter. Surely the deeper teaching of all Christian groups leads to valuing social peace above imposing beliefs on one another. If Christians can institutionalize such peace only by transferring the focus of practical commitment to nations, then they must support the resulting nationalism.

Obviously, this religious and spiritual change did not occur abruptly in the middle of the seventeenth century. Looking back one can see many developments in the preceding centuries leading to nationalism. The competition between Spain and Portugal for the conquest and settlement of Latin America was surely nationalist. Nevertheless, the church played a large role. Also, the conquest required justification in Christianist terms. Nor should we suppose that the appeals to Christian warrants were mere window dressing. They were important for the rulers of Spain and Portugal and even for many of the conquistadores.

On the other side, after the establishment of nationalism, many states continued to seek legitimation from Christian teaching and even from their relation to churches. For millions of people to this day, primary devotion continues to be to Christianity or to the God Christianity proclaims. The great missionary movement of the nineteenth century understood itself in terms more of Christian faith than of nationalism, even if in fact it often served nationalistic ends. Even now political leaders often appeal for legitimation to Christianity.

Nevertheless, the change that occurred in the middle of the seventeenth century was profound. Since then, in the West, the power of the churches has been clearly subordinated to the state. Few among even the most devoted Christian believers would want it otherwise. Increasingly the states have forced the churches to live side by side, no one church claiming the right to determine matters of faith for all citizens.

In this changed situation, the legitimation of the state, formerly sought in Christian teaching and church practice, was grounded in a new story of origins. This story depicted an original world in which each individual was totally free. This freedom included the freedom to take whatever one wanted from one's neighbor if one were strong enough to do so. This might include taking the neighbor's life. In short this freedom entailed an anarchy in which all were at war with all others. To escape this miserable condition, all entered into a compact to surrender their individual freedom in exchange for imposed security. In this way the nation state came into being. From this story, the state could claim rightful authority as long as it maintained internal order. It did not need Christian sanction.

During the following centuries wars were fought on a larger scale than ever before. Often all the nations involved claimed that God was on their side. The churches usually gave nations the support they desired. When there were religious differences between the nations at war, these fueled the intensity of national feeling. But the wars were fought by nations for the power, the glory, and the wealth of the nation. Millions of people have willingly given their lives for the sake of their nations.

If more justification was required for war, this was formulated in political terms. A people might claim the right of self-determination, which is the right to be an independent nation. French aggression at the beginning of the nineteenth

century was in the name of the political rights of ordinary
citizens.

Each nation had its own self-glorifying history. That of the
United States stressed the escape from persecution in Europe,
the establishment of freedom in the New World, the glorious
struggle for independence from the remaining tyranny of
England, the formation of a new nation that achieved and
defended its national sovereignty against many threats, the
settlement and civilization of the frontier, the offering of refuge
and opportunity to the suffering masses of Europe, the rise to
international power, and the support of democracy against
tyranny everywhere.

Many Christians recognized that nationalism had assumed
the role of religion. Although the great majority subordinated
their church commitments to their national ones, those for
whom Christian faith was truly a devotion to God that relativized all other loyalties criticized nationalism. A few refused to
serve their countries in war out of this higher loyalty. Many
more saw in this loyalty a reason to seek international cooperation and even some transfer of power from national governments to international ones.

This critique of nationalism, to which Christianity contributed, prepared the ground for the League of Nations and,
later, the United Nations, as well as the World Court. But it
would be an exaggeration to see these institutions as having
displaced nationalism. They were accepted because most
nations came to see them as in their national interest. Nations
as nations continue to be the actors within them, and the more
powerful nations, such as the United States, make sure
that they are not bound by international decisions they do not
like.

I have emphasized the positive role played by nationalism
in making possible mutual toleration among Christians with
divergent beliefs and practices. Nations also performed many
other positive functions. They gradually replaced churches as
the major agencies of care for the destitute and provision of
education and health services for the masses. They became
more open to the influence of ordinary people than the major
churches had been during the Christianist period.

Unfortunately, the support garnered by nations through
their many public services was often channelled into aggressive

behavior in relation to the rest of the world. Furthermore, it was often strengthened by myths of racial purity and cultural superiority and by celebrations of national history that portrayed other nations as villains. These negative features were intensified in Germany by the Nazis, so that the German Reich became a caricature of nationalism.

Its nationalism led Germany to the extermination of those peoples, chiefly the Jews, who were thought to contaminate its national purity. It also led it to a war of conquest throughout Europe. The resultant horrors showed the depths of the evil brought about by unchecked nationalism. After World War II it was not possible to reorganize Western Europe on purely nationalist principles.

IV. FROM NATIONALISM TO ECONOMISM

One check on nationalism instituted at the end of World War II was the United Nations (UN). But this by no means signaled the end of nationalism. The reorganization of Europe itself was more important. This reorganization was under the rubric of the European Economic Community.

The shift from Christianism to nationalism in the mid-seventeenth century is parallelled by a shift from nationalism to economism in the mid-twentieth. The emergence of the European Economic Community is a sign of this shift. It has worked progressively, and with considerable success, to unify Europe into a single market for the sake of the prosperity of the whole. Of course, it repeatedly encounters obstacles in the residual nationalism of some of its members. But these are generally viewed as remnants of an earlier culture not appropriate to the world into which we are moving. European national governments are expected to make those decisions that are needed for the economic prosperity of the people of Europe. National power and glory should be subordinated to this economic goal.

World War II did not mark the end of United States' nationalism in the same way. The war did not cause suffering in the US comparable to that in Europe. Few thought of American nationalism as belonging to the same genus as German nationalism. Hence it was not discredited in the American mind. Instead, the nation was thought to have a new mission to lead the world to democracy and prosperity.

Pursuing these goals, the United States led in the creation of the United Nations, on the one side, and the Bretton Woods institutions (BWI) – the IMF and the World Bank – on the other. Closely related, a little later, there emerged the General Agreement on Tariffs and Trade (GATT), which has now developed into the World Trade Organization (WTO). One may argue that these organizations were means of exerting US national power and thus an expression of American nationalism. Yet it is significant, even under that interpretation, that most of the means of exerting national power were recognized as economic.

These organizations collectively were created in order to further trade throughout the world and, thereby, economic prosperity. This involves reducing the ability of national governments to regulate their own economies. The assumption is that all people will be better off if market forces replace national policies as the primary determinants of international trade.

The BWI have been remarkably successful. This is not only because of their own skill but also because the economistic ideology has become more and more widely accepted. National governments are now willing (or forced) to give up the right to regulate national economies for the sake of participating in global economic growth. 'Protectionism,' which was standard economic procedure prior to World War II, and has been widely practiced since then by such successful countries as Japan, South Korea, and Taiwan, is now taken as self-evidently evil. The world is moving toward the global market that is the fulfillment of the economistic dream.

Not only has the United States been the leading actor in shaping this global economism, it has also adopted an internal order that is correctly described as economistic. The reasoning is the same. Governmental interference in the economy renders it less efficient. Without greater efficiency it cannot compete effectively in the new global market. Hence the US government surrenders some of its authority over its own economy, including the boundaries of its national market, for the sake of increasing economic prosperity. Within the United States as within Europe, economism triumphs.

Economism has come to dominance in US thinking about Third World development. In the first decades after World War II, development thinking included humanitarian elements that related to Third World societies more broadly. The Peace Corps was the most idealistic expression of this vision. Subsequently Cold War considerations became a major determinant. But during the Reagan administration, development came to be identified with economic growth to be achieved by private investments by transnational corporations (TNCs).

Foreign policy with regard to neighbors also came to be dominated by economistic considerations. Reducing barriers to investment and trade has been the primary goal. This was worked out first with Canada and subsequently extended and expanded into the North American Free Trade Agreement (NAFTA). Each government gives up some of its rights to regulate some of its internal affairs for the sake of a larger market intended to encourage economic growth throughout the region. The Clinton administration now wants to extend the free trade zone to all of Latin America.

How far this surrender of national power goes depends on how the courts interpret the provisions of NAFTA. At this writing 'the Ethyl Corporation is suing the Canadian government for $251 million over the Canadian Parliament's banning of MMT (a toxic fuel additive), as an infringement of its rights. The government is concerned over the effects of MMT on the health, environment and automobile emission control devices. Ethyl argues that such measures are "tantamount to expropriation."'[1]

Another indication of the shift from nationalism to economism in US foreign policy is its relative support for the international organizations (especially the UN) in comparison with the global economic ones. Support for the UN has waxed and waned, but overall the US has used its power to weaken the ability of the UN to influence global economic matters. Control over these has been transferred progressively to the BWI and the WTO. The tendency of the General Assembly of the UN to give weight to the national interests of Third World nations interfered with the smooth transition to the global market run on economistic principles; so the US has done much to weaken the General Assembly.

Further, it is significant that when the rulers of seven major powers meet annually, this has been known as the Economic Summit. It is now assumed that the primary reason for national leaders to discuss their differences and shared concerns is economic. Their pronouncements consistently support economistic policies.

At this writing, the move toward disempowering national governments with regard to their internal economic life is proceding still further. The Organization for Economic Cooperation and Development (OECD) is negotiating a Multilateral Agreement on Investments (MAI). The original intention was to include this in the Uruguay Round of the GATT that led to the creation of WTO. But resistance by Third World nations to some of its provisions caused the omission of MAI. Formulation of the agreement was shifted to the OECD which is composed of industrialized countries more supportive of the transfer of power to economic actors.

In its current form the agreement disallows any restrictions on international capital flows. It 'calls for the ban of "performance requirements." Performance requirements are conditions, such as paying a living wage or adhering to certain environmental standards, that a government may put on an approval of an investment, such as the opening of a new factory. The MAI would also require "absolute national treatment." In other words, foreign corporations and investors would be required to be treated equally or better than domestic corporations and investors. These rules would be enforced by a new corporate right to directly sue governments for monetary damages if they believe they have not received all the benefits promised by the treaty.'[2]

As long as some remnants of the earlier nationalism are in force, corporations can sue governments only in the courts of the country in question and only according to its laws. The MAI changes that. Disputes between corporations and governments will be resolved by a panel at the International Center for the Settlement of Investment Disputes(ICSID), a branch of the World Bank family, appeal to which, in the past, has been voluntary. The corporation and the government will play an equal role in determining membership on this panel. There is no recourse from its decisions. This status of corporations as officially equal to national governments in power and rights is a continuation and extension of what has already been developed in the WTO and NAFTA.

Currently there are moves within the UN also to recognize the high status of the TNCs. Since the UN was set up strictly to represent governments, the full inclusion of TNCs in decision making has been resisted. Indeed, for some years it had a Center on TNCs and proposed to write a code of conduct for them. TNC pressure brought an end to this effort and led to closing the Center.

The move now is to formalize corporate involvement in the UN decision-making process. This is expected to take place under the auspices of the Commission on Sustainable Development. David Korten attended a meeting on 24 June 1997 designed to advance this process. He reports that 'Mr Kofi Annan, Secretary General of the UN, gave the corporate CEOs a warm welcome with his message that he sees opportunities for the private sector and the UN cooperating at many levels...He praised UNDP for its role in preparing the way for private investment to come into Third World countries and called on governments to provide incentives to move business in this direction.'[3]

The apparent reason for formalizing the already great influence of the TNCs is that they have far more money available to invest than do national governments. If they participate in setting the rules, these will be more acceptable to them, and more money will flow. Their high status in an economistic world is assured by the fact that 'of the world's 100 largest economies, 51 are corporations. Only 49 are countries.'[4]

With all these changes it has become clear that the nature and the role of the state must be rethought. It is striking that the lead in this thinking is coming from an institution established to promote economic development. The World Bank devoted its *World Development Report 1997* to 'The State in a Changing World.'[5] It has found that the efforts of states to promote economic development have often gone awry, and it has itself done much to reduce the capacity of states to engage in these mistaken practices.

The Bank notes now that states have far less freedom to determine basic economic policies. 'Taxes, investment rules, and economic policies must be ever more responsive to the paramenters of a globalized world economy.'[6] Since the state is no longer to manage its own economic life, and since it is the global market that plays the primary role in development, the state must be redefined in terms of its supporting functions and of alleviating the human and environmental costs of the working of the autonomous economic system.

V. THE OVERLAP OF EPOCHS

Just as dating the shift from Christianism to nationalism at the middle of the seventeenth century is too simple, so also is dating the shift to economism in the middle of the twentieth century. Obviously this shift was possible only because economics had played a very large role for a long time before. Even in the epoch of Christianism the economy was of utmost importance in shaping the feudal system, in the creation of city states, and in the rise of nations. No doubt it played some role in the Crusades and in the division of Christendom between Catholicism and Protestantism.

What can be said with some confidence, however, is that during that period, one who justified greed because of its contribution to the growth of the economy would not have gained a hearing. More generally, one who appealed to economic gain alone as the reason for changing social policy would have been regarded as eccentric. The benefit of the society as a whole was the goal of social policy, and how such benefit was to be understood was determined primarily by Christian teaching. Of course, having sufficient goods properly distributed was of great importance to society. But one would not argue for change simply on the grounds that it would increase the quantity of goods if that same policy would be disruptive of the existing social order.

In the nationalist epoch the importance of the economy grew. One of the main contributors to national power and glory was the national economy. Empires were conquered and colonies were established to enhance the national wealth. Nations developed both external and internal policies for the purpose of enhancing this wealth.

The rise of modern economic theory was in this context. Adam Smith's classic book was on 'The Wealth of Nations.'[7] It provided advice as to how a nation could increase its wealth. The early argument for free trade was that it served to increase national wealth.

Karl Polanyi showed that during the eighteenth century a basic change took place in the relation of the economy to local communities.[8] Prior to that time it was assumed that the economy was a part of local communities and functioned to serve them. After that time it came to be understood that the national economy was served better when markets ceased to be local. That meant that local communities were required to adjust to the needs of a larger market. The power of the economy to shape affairs internal to nations was well developed in the period of nationalism.

The next step was the application to nations of the same logic earlier applied to local communities. It was this step that was taken after World War II. Nations, too, were to subordinate themselves to the service of the market.

Although liberal and neo-liberal economics through the nineteenth century tended to take national boundaries as given, Marxist theory did not. It affirmed economics as the primary determinant of history. For it, national governments were instruments of the bourgeoisie in fulfilling their economic goals. Marxism thus offered an economistic view of history. Many believers in Marxism accepted this interpretation and gave their personal commitment to economic goals rather than to national ones.

Nevertheless, history proved Marx wrong or, more exactly, proved wrong those who tried to implement his goals prematurely. At the time of World War I, Marxists expected the solidarity of workers in France and Germany against their capitalist exploiters to be stronger than their national feeling. But it was not so. Although many felt exploited by capitalists, both French and German workers still fought for their respective nations. National feeling was stronger than class feeling. Where Communism won power, especially in the Soviet Union, it subordinated the goals of transnational Communism to the strengthening of national power.

This means that Communism did not play a large role in the actual supplanting of nationalism by economism. This was accomplished much more by capitalism and by the economic theory that describes, supports, and directs it. Hence the shift from primary concern for national wealth to focus on the global market did not take place until after World War II.

Just as economics played an enormous role in the West during the period of nationalism, so also national loyalties are still a potent force in the context of the victory of economism. In the US the current mood is away from internationalism. Many are deeply committed to maintaining national military might and exercising it with little regard to allies or to the UN.

Despite this nationalist opposition to international political and military cooperation, there is no effective political resistance to the transfer of national power to transnational economic institutions, public or private. As long as such transfer is held to create jobs and increase prosperity, opposition falls away. Purely nationalistic arguments about the importance of national sovereignty over the national economy are heard hardly more than Christian ones. When voiced by Patrick Buchanan, they are ridiculed as irrelevant.[9] The change that has occurred in this regard is striking.

NOTES

1. Don E. McAlister, e-mail communication, 14 July 1997.
2. 'Public Citizen Liberates Secret Treaty,' *Public Citizen*, Spring 1997, p.14.
3. David Korten, 'The United Nations and the Corporate Agenda,' e-mail communication, 2 July 1997.
4. Doug Hinrichs and David Roodman, 'Economic Globalization: An interview with David Korten,' *Ecological Economics Bulletin*, Vol. 2, No. 3, Third Quarter 1997, p.14.
5. Washington: World Bank, 1997.
6. *Summary: The State in a Changing World*. Washington: World Bank, 1997, p. 2.
7. (1776) New York: Random House.
8. Karl Polanyi, *The Great Transformation*. Boston: Beacon Press, 1957.
9. See Patrick I. Buchanan, *The Great Betrayal: How American Sovereignty and Social Justice are Being Sacrificed to the Gods of the Global Economy*. Boston: Little, Brown and Co., 1998. Note especially his account of his reception at the Cato Institute, p. 19.

2 Economism and the Challenge of Earthism

I. THE FAITH OF ECONOMISM

Economism is the belief that primary devotion should be directed to the expansion of the economy. According to the dominant economistic theory, large markets allow for greater specialization and economies of scale along with adequate competition to establish optimum prices. The ideal is a global market. This can be attained only as national boundaries cease to inhibit the flow of goods and capital. That means the control over this flow by nation states should be reduced and even eliminated. It also means that within each state, government's role is to encourage competition among the economic actors, local and international, and to provide the infrastructure that enables business to prosper.

Economistic thinkers believe that the growth of production achieved in this way will solve the most important of the world's problems. Without this conviction, there would be no justification for giving priority to economic growth over all other considerations. But if, indeed, human well-being, as understood by a wide range of variables, is enhanced by economic growth and cannot be dealt with as well in other ways, then those concerned for human well-being should accept the primacy of the economic order. The real issue, from this perspective, is only which economistic ideology and practice should be adopted.

The most obvious claim of economism is that economic growth improves the general economic well-being of people. Economists consider in each situation how better to meet the desires of some without doing harm to any. Economistic thinkers see growth as coming close to fulfilling this requirement. Market transactions are voluntary, and people do not voluntarily exchange goods or services unless they benefit from the exchange. If some lose out in market competition, a growing economy allows society to prevent this failure from being humanly devastating by providing some kind of safety net. Hence, it is claimed, economic growth contributes to the economic well-being of people generally.

Secondly, economic growth is held to be the way of overcoming poverty without the use of force. The alternative solution to poverty would be redistribution of goods, and since those who are better off do not voluntarily give up their goods, this requires an authoritarian government ready to use force. On the other hand, if the economic pie grows larger, each group's share of the pie, if it remains the same fraction, increases in size. The poor gain along with other segments of society rather than at their expense. This makes possible improvement of their lot, it is asserted, along with the maintenance of social harmony.

Third, economic growth is believed to create jobs and so work toward full-employment. It is true that full-employment can be attained by government make-work programs. But the growing market creates jobs that are useful to society and, therefore, meaningful to the worker. Although individual employers may downsize and thus put employees out of work, the greater efficiency that results makes capital available for other productive investment. This generates new jobs, so that employment overall increases.

Fourth, it is affirmed that economic growth leads to better pay and working conditions. The more efficient use of capital involves increasing the productivity of labor, that is, the amount produced per hour of work. As productivity rises, wages also rise. Workers demand more healthful working conditions and get them.

Fifth, it is argued that economic growth makes possible improvements in health and education. An affluent society has the resources to address these important dimensions of human well-being. People who have met their basic needs demand these services.

Sixth, economic growth is claimed to solve the problem of excessive increase in population. When average income reaches a certain point, it is said, family size diminishes. This may be because children who are an economic asset in poor societies are an economic burden in affluent ones. In any case, this 'population transition' can be documented in Europe and elsewhere. It is asserted that, for this reason, no government interference with private matters is needed to achieve population stability.

Seventh, economic growth is believed to solve the environmental problem as well. In poor societies the urgency of survival needs is such that no attention can be paid to preservation of environmental amenities. But when economic growth satisfies basic needs, environmental quality becomes a priority. Economically prosperous societies, it is asserted, are motivated to deal with these matters and have the resources to do so.

Eighth, it is claimed that the market activities that make for economic growth also lead to democratic governments and civil rights. Freedom in the market leads to the demand for political freedoms and for participation in political processes. The entrepreneurial class is especially concerned to extend its rights from the economic order to the political one. Free markets, according to this argument, lead to free elections, representative democracies, and civil rights.

If these claims are justified, then wholehearted concentration on quantitative growth of production should suffice as the focus of activity of those committed to human well-being. No special attention need be given to any of these other issues. Whatever global system leads most effectively to growth should be adopted.

II. ECONOMISTIC HISTORIES

Economism, like nationalism and Christianism, provides its self-justifying account of history. According to this story, through most of human history most people lived close to the edge of survival. The vast majority worked as peasants and produced little more than they needed for their own subsistence. What more they did produce was taken from them to support the political-military-priestly elite. When conditions were good, population would grow, but when weather or social conditions were unfavorable, many would die.

The great change came with the industrial revolution. This enabled workers to produce much more than they needed to survive. At first this surplus was taken from them, but in the new context it was invested in other facilities that increased production still more. Eventually, total production grew so much that there were surplus goods for all. This made possible the rapid rise of the standard of living for the masses of people.

For the first time in history, most people lived far above the level of mere subsistence and survival. A quality of life that had formerly been possible only for the few came to be taken for granted by people generally. Standards of health and well-being generally rose dramatically. What happened in the industrialized nations of the West is now occurring globally. The implication of this account is clearly that all other considerations should be subordinated to the growth of the global economy.

To draw the full implications, however, more detail is required. In the Marxist telling, the emphasis is on the exploitation of labor built into the capitalist system. Even when workers receive better compensation, Marxists assert that much of the fruit of their labor is transferred to capitalists. Also, in part, the prosperity of labor in the First World has been due to exploitation of workers in the Third World.

At the same time the Marxist account recognizes that this exploitative capitalist system leads to rapid growth without which the economistic goal of plenty for all cannot be reached. Capitalism also leads to the concentration of the means of production in fewer and fewer hands. In the purest form of the story, the implication is that workers should wait until capitalism has performed its function of drastic increase of production, has concentrated ownership in a few hands, and then take over from those few in the name of all the workers whose exploitation has made this vast production possible.

When the accent is on exploitation, however, the story has been heard more often in another way. It implies that the system is so unjust that all those who are being exploited should rise up against their oppressors and seize power from them. They can manage the increase of production themselves.

When the history of the world is told by advocates of capitalism, on the other hand, the term exploitation disappears except for egregious instances. Instead, one reads not only of workers but also of investors and entrepreneurs, all of whose contributions are essential to the growth that in turn benefits all. In this telling, the enemy is often government when it undertakes to play roles for which it is not qualified. For example, if government sets prices, this distorts production in the direction of higher priced goods which may not be needed, whereas the market prices goods according to actual demand. Similarly, if government interferes in establishing wages for labor, this is likely to slow the growth which lower labor costs facilitate. Finally, excessive taxing of profits reduces funds available for new investments and thus slows the growth through which the whole society gains.

Some histories give equal weight to the distorting effects of monopolies or cartels. These also can take pricing and wages out of the hands of the free market. Today, unfortunately, this part of the story is often muted.

Subtle differencs in the story can lead to support of different policies. But many of the implications of the dominant capitalist account are clear. Government intervention is to be minimized in favor of allowing markets to set prices and thus allocate resources efficiently. Entrepreneurs are to be prized as the agents of progress and should therefore receive appropriate rewards. Investors are of utmost importance; so the presence of the rich should be celebrated. Local markets should be integrated into larger ones.

III. STRENGTHS AND WEAKNESSES OF ECONOMISM

Chapter 1 emphasized the positive gains involved in the rise of nationalism as well as its ultimate failures. It is clear that there are analogous gains and failures in economism. We will consider first the gains, but balance them with comments on their limitations and the problems generated by economism.

One great gain is that the shift from nationalism to economism has virtually ensured that the Western powers will not again draw the world into nationalistic wars among themselves. Further, when the Soviet Union finally succumbed to economic pressures, the danger of a global military conflict between East and West also greatly subsided. No major industrial power is now likely to go to war against another. The interdependence of the economies of almost all countries, along with the economistic spirit that dominates, renders this almost unthinkable.

Economism has offered another great advantage. The economic growth at which it aims has reduced class conflict in the industrialized nations. In a stagnant economy, resentment of the rich by the working class is likely. Marx understood the dynamics of history around the conflict between these classes. He believed this conflict was greatly intensified by capitalism and that, as capitalism concentrated more and more wealth in fewer and fewer hands, it would eventually destroy itself.

It turned out, however, that capitalism could develop in such a way that the wealth it created could be widely shared. As long as workers anticipated improvement of their lot within the system, they were rarely disposed to make basic changes in the system. In the phrase made famous by John F. Kennedy, 'a rising tide lifts all ships.' Workers sometimes struggle to increase their share of the pie, but they do so within the system.

Economistic theory recognizes that at certain stages of economic growth, wealth may be concentrated in fewer hands, but it also holds that in time the growing pie will allow all slices to be larger. During the first decades of the economistic period, the economic condition of workers in the First World did improve remarkably, and many Third World countries advanced rapidly in economic terms. Where this occurred, revolutionary ideologies had little success.

On the other hand, economism values people entirely by their contribution to the market. In most countries some people do not fit into the market. Thus there develops an underclass of excluded persons. These usually contribute disproportionately to disease, violence, and the destructive use of drugs. The self-destructive practices of many of them lead to loss of support from the working poor. Their future, accordingly, is precarious. The end of conflict between workers and capitalists has been succeeded by a deep and unhealthy separation between those who participate in the market and those who do not.

Furthermore, the economic growth fostered by economism is often experienced as exploitative by the poor in Third World countries. Their small landholdings are taken away for the sake of more efficient production by agribusiness. They are removed from their homes so that large areas can be flooded by dams. Their labor unions are weakened so that wages can be kept 'competitive.' Their forest commons are cut down and sold for lumber.

Often they resist. To suppress such resistance, the military, in the service of economism, has developed a characteristic form of warfare called 'low intensity conflict.' It is often accompanied by campaigns of terror waged against those who speak out for the interests of the poor. In short, international war was replaced by a new kind of class warfare in many countries, especially in Latin America. The United States established the School of the Americas to instruct Latin American military leaders in the waging of such wars.

There are other evils of the earlier nationalism that economism reduces. One is parochialism. More and more people think in global terms. They are aware of what is occurring in other parts of the world. They think of other peoples less as inferior or exotic and more as similar to themselves and as participants with them in an integrated global market. Many are now personally acquainted with individuals of other cultures and religions. They are less vulnerable to the negative caricatures so common in the Christianist and nationalist periods. The triumph of economism reduces the danger to such minorities as the Jews, who suffered so terribly from both Christianism and nationalism.

On the other hand, in many parts of the world economism plays an unwelcome imperialist role. It has shaped the dominant global reality, so that almost all nations are subject to its rule. But there are large parts of the world that have not shared the religious history of the West and have not, therefore, inwardly succumbed to its wiles.

The most globally significant religious alternative to economism today is Islam, or more realistically, Islamism. There are hundreds of millions of people whose attitude toward Islam today is much like that of Christians toward Christianity in the age of Christianism. It provides them their identity and offers a supreme loyalty.

Of course, among them there are many who, in authentically Islamic fashion, worship Allah and give only secondary loyalty to Islam as such. But Islamism has most of the positive and negative features that once characterized Christianism. It is a more powerful force in many countries than either nationalism or economism, and it can provide a focus of loyalty around which to rally against the ravages of economism.

Whereas economism tends to reduce hostility among religions and cultures which do not interfere with its goals, it can lead to considerable hostility to competing commitments such as Islamism. It can understand this only as fundamentalism and fanaticism. Since it happens that many Muslims live in just that part of the world that is best endowed with the oil that fuels the economistic machine, their different commitments cannot be ignored by economistic thinkers. Economism does not insure freedom from conflict with the Islamic world!

Just as nationalism delivered on the promise of social order, allowing persons of differing faiths to live together in peace, so economism has delivered on its promise to create more goods and services per capita worldwide. Despite rapid population growth, during the past fifty years global economic growth has vastly exceeded population growth. There are billions of people who are more prosperous today than were their forebears in the years before and immediately after World War II. Few of them would willingly give up these gains.

On the other hand, these gains have been made at great cost to the environment. Also, the system used to speed growth typically undermines traditional communities and means of subsistence. It generates thereby among some sectors of the population a form of misery rare in past history. Economism as such does nothing to replace the personal, moral, and spiritual support and nurture traditional communities have provided in the past. Nihilistic and anti-social attitudes become more widespread.

IV. THE RISE OF EARTHISM

The degradation of the Earth and the destruction of those human communities that have lived closest to it have evoked innumerable protests. Most of these have been fragmentary and isolated. But their unity and coherence has become increasingly visible. They constitute a new global force that challenges economism. This can be called Earthism. Although some concern for the Earth has characterized the West throughout its history, Earthism is a new phenomenon arising in reaction to economism.

During the Christianist epoch there was no sharp line of division between human artifacts and the natural world. Since that world was vast in comparison with the humanly constructed world, it was assumed that it would take care of itself, or more accurately, that God's providence included the whole of divine creation. No one doubted that human well-being depended on the soil and its fruits.

During the nationalist era attention was focused chiefly on ethnic groups. But in most instances such groups identified themselves also with the landscape that constituted their homeland. Strong feelings were directed both to the people and to their land. The England that evoked unselfish devotion from so many was not only the English people, it was also their island home.

Economism, however, has split this bond of people and land. Originally modern economists spoke of land along with labor and capital as a factor of production, but this meant only the contribution of the soil to agricultural production. Even this disappeared from economic thinking. Land was assimilated to capital or treated as a commodity.

Since land was the only category under which nature appeared in economic theory, this meant that the natural world ceased to be consdidered. Those who view the world through the lens of economic theory, whether capitalist or Marxist, regard the specific conditions of the natural world as unimportant. Of course, some notice is given to natural resources, but they are treated as though other forms of capital can substitute for them or as though they can be substituted indefinitely for one another. Accordingly economists feel no need for empirical investigation of physical conditions in order to develop and apply their theories.

When economic goals became globally dominant, the resulting economistic theory continued to focus on capital and labor to the exclusion of nature. What is prized is the transformation of natural resources into artificial products. Wealth is measured in terms of these products alone. In short, nature disappears from view. As a result, policies based on economic theory are insenstive to their effects on the natural world.

This dominant preoccupation with the artificial world has made those who care about nature keenly conscious of this concern. For the first time in human history the living system on the surface of the planet appears seriously threatened by human activity. Yet this fact is ignored or denied by the dominant faith. This situation has called forth a passionate reaction. Many realize in a quite new way their devotion to the now threatened Earth.

Earlier everyone had some concern both about what humans fashioned and about nature. There were certainly differences of emphasis, but there was no sharp polarization. Now that economism has arisen with its total focus on the artificial, those who care about nature have reacted with an opposite focus on the natural world, intensified by their sense of its fragility and vulnerability to human actions. This new situation gives rise to Earthism.

Earthists see that in some ways theirs is a recurrence to ways of thinking that were characteristic of hunting and gathering people. Indeed the spirituality of Earthism draws on these ancient traditions. Earthists find there a reverence for the Earth and an appreciation for human beings as fitting into the patterns of the Earth that was lost in all the historic cultures and religions and has been most systematically rejected in economism.

But Earthism is not a recurrence to primal religious thinking or sensibility. This was formed in a context in which the natural world was the dominant reality and human beings were both nurtured and threatened by it. It embodied its own science, but this was very different from the modern one. Contemporary Earthists experience the relation of human activity and the Earth quite differently, and their understanding of the Earth relies extensively on modern and post-modern science.

Some Earthists take extreme positions, seeming to be misanthropic in their horror over what human beings are doing to other creatures. But in fact it is not possible for them to ignore human beings in the way economism ignores the natural world. They are themselves human, and the Earth they celebrate and reverence includes them. Earthists know that the human species is an important and valuable part of the whole, and they argue that it should recognize this fact and act accordingly, respectful of the other parts of the system, animate and inanimate.

Economistic thinkers assume that the one goal is the satisfaction of human wants. If they find that some humans want nature to be healthy, they will try to find how much they are willing to pay for this end. Thus the condition of nature can be assigned monetary value and in that way can enter the economistic system. Hence, it is an exaggeration to say that economistic thinking takes *no* account of the natural world. But this way of considering the significance of nature is offensive to Earthists.

Still, the difference is sharp. Earthists are offended at the economistic valuing of the Earth only in terms of what people would pay to preserve it. They see the health of the Earth, including its human inhabitants, as of supreme importance. They recognize human economic activity as one important element in that system, but they see it as having assumed an altogether inappropriate predominance. Instead of dominating the Earth, the economy should serve the well-being of the system as a whole. Doing so certainly includes meeting human needs. But the goal is to meet those needs in ways that disrupt and degrade the overall system as little as possible.

Another way of putting the contrast is in terms of top-down and bottom-up thinking. Economistic thinkers typically seek to expand human economic activity as much as possible so as to create as much artifical wealth as they can. The process of doing so directly enriches the major economic actors, but as they become richer, wealth is supposed to trickle down to the poor. Believers in the dominant ideology think that this wealth can satisfy human desires including the desire for preserving bits of nature. Earthists typically seek the regeneration of natural systems and focus attention on those human beings who live most intimately with these systems. The health of these systems improves the livelihood of those who live in and from them, and their improved economic condition provides a basis for the livelihood also of those who are more remote, usually city dwellers.

In general the application of economistic policies concentrates population in megalopolises. The application of Earthist principles leads to decentralization. Economism calls for the globalization of the market. Earthism favors emphasis on local markets. Economism leads to development policies that emphasize large infrastructure projects requiring technical skills and capital investment far beyond the capacity of local people. Earthism emphasizes projects which are decided on by local people and which they can participate in carrying out. Economism seeks national and global strategies. Earthism favors community development. Economistic policies concentrate the control of the global economic process in fewer and fewer hands. Earthist policies lead to local control of local economies.

Economistic thinkers typically believe that there is no problem about the indefinite expansion of the economy. Indeed, this indefinite expansion is their goal. They meet the warnings of physical scientists with skepticism. History has shown to their satisfaction that the technology that is such an important part of capital can solve the many problems that natural limits are supposed to put in the way of continuing economic growth. They point to many past instances that illustrate this.

Earthist thinkers take the warning of physical scientists with great seriousness. Even if there should prove to be no physical limits to economic growth, they deplore the effects on the Earth, and especially on the people who live closest to the land, of the growth that has already occurred. They deplore the mindset that sees these negative effects as insignificant in comparison to the positive values of the rapid expansion of industrial production. In any case their sensitivity to the condition of the Earth-system leads them to believe that there are indeed limits to its ability to provide resources and absorb wastes. Limits to growth appear to them to be evident realities that economism ignores to the peril of all forms of life.

Earthism does not deny that economic growth can have some of the benefits it claims. Nations with larger per capita incomes do tend to have less extreme poverty and unemployment, better wages and working conditions, and better health care and education. In general, population growth is slower in these countries and more attention is paid to the environment.

Nevertheless, Earthists are not impressed by these claims. The human condition which is measured in these ways can be improved equally or more by other policies than those that aim at economic growth. In most of the world, prospects of ever attaining sufficient per capita income for these matters to take care of themselves are remote. Meanwhile, the immediate effects of growth-oriented policies cut in just the opposite direction.

Earthism is the one spiritual force in the West now able to challenge economism. From time to time it has succeeded in checking particular economistic policies. At Montréal, for example, despite opposition from some economistic thinkers, leading nations agreed to reduce their production of chemicals that threaten the ozone layer.

Pressures from Earthists led the United Nations to organize the Earth Summit at Rio de Janeiro in 1992. Some hoped that this might signal the shift from the dominance of economism to that of Earthism. It did not. Under the leadership of the United States, economism triumphed. Nevertheless, there were some concessions to Earthism.

Even economistic thinkers want economic growth to be sustainable. Where Earthists can point out convincingly that particular patterns of economic growth are not sustainable, economistic thinkers concede that changes are needed. Their commitment is that these changes not interfere with the economistic project of a growing global economy.

The influence of Earthism has led to a shift in rhetoric from 'economic growth' to 'sustainable development.' Among economistic thinkers, this means sustainable economic growth as measured by standard national accounts such as Gross Domestic Product (GDP). Their assumption is that economic growth continues to be the end toward which policies are properly directed. But when Earthists point toward changes that can make this growth easier to continue, they accept them. Greater efficiency in the use of energy, for example, is acceptable in this context.

Moderate Earthists work closely with moderate economistic thinkers to find win-win situations. That is, they seek changes that will both bring greater profits to corporations over a longer period of time and also reduce the pressure on natural resources and sinks for pollution. Fortunately, there are many such projects. As long as the focus in kept on these, the difference of commitment and concern can be kept in the background.

Other Earthists, however, are convinced that the more fundamental issues cannot be ignored. The top-down growth-oriented economy continues to degrade the Earth even if at a somewhat slower pace than would be the case if technological improvements were not introduced. The goal of increased consumption in affluent countries must be directly challenged, so that technological improvements can be used to give space for growth in poor countries. Policies should be directed to the regeneration of nature rather than simply to slowing down its decay. Population growth must be slowed everywhere, so that the effort to meet basic human needs of all can be realized without destructive increases in production. There is no sign that Rio marks the beginning of an Earthist age. On the contrary, the commitment to economic growth and the pressure of the resultant activities on the Earth-system are themselves growing. Earthists view 'sustainable economic growth' as an oxymoron. The physical system of the Earth as a whole sets limits to the economic subsystem that grows within it.

V. PROSPECTS

The previous chapter emphasized the overlapping of epochs. Nation states had developed a long way under the dominance of Christianism before nationalism succeeded Christianism as the dominant force. Economic institutions had assumed enormous importance during the nationalistic era long before they replaced nation states as the primary actors on the world scene. Worldwide there are growing protests against what economism is doing to the Earth, and with increasing frequency these gain coherent articulation in Earthist forms. Earthists can hope that before it is too late there will come a tilt in which Earthism supersedes economism as the dominant force. If that happens, there will be global efforts to subordinate economic activity to the well-being of the Earth and all its inhabitants.

Examination of what was required to end the Christianist and nationalist eras, however, is not encouraging with respect to what would have to occur to bring about the victory of Earthism. Christianism had done much harm over a long period of time without engendering a serious threat to its dominance. It took thirty years of fratricidal conflict in the heart of Europe to bring its hegemony to an end. Nationalism had done enormous harm throughout the world for centuries without bringing about a serious threat to its dominance. It took two World Wars, and especially the caricature of nationalism in German National Socialism, to undermine its spiritual dominion.

In Earthist eyes the destruction wrought in the world by economism in the past few decades is enormous. It has uprooted millions of peoples, separated hundreds of millions from their traditional communities, increased crime, addiction, and family breakdown, slaughtered many of the poor in low intensity conflicts, decimated the world's forest cover, depleted its fisheries, eroded much of its topsoil, and speeded up the loss of biodiversity. It is changing the world's climate in ways that are likely to cause critical problems for our grandchildren.

None of this has thus far affected its spiritual and practical hegemony. On the contrary its domination of mind and heart around the world is increasing. It has persuaded hundreds of millions of the poor that, despite present suffering and long delays, its policies offer the one hope that they will one day share in the affluence they see on television. Meanwhile it increases the wealth of the affluent.

It has led most people to concentrate attention with it on the artificial world it is enlarging rather than on the natural basis it is eroding. It uses economistic ways of measuring success to persuade the public that its policies are moving the world in the right direction even when actual experience suggests something quite different. Its experts assure all questioners that the problems identified by Earthists are not serious, that the methods being employed by economism will solve them. The real problem, they argue, is the remaining resistance to the total triumph of economism arising from nationalism on the one side and Earthism on the other.

The economistic message gives hope to the poor and comfort to the affluent, and it supports the rich in the concentration of wealth in their own hands. No wonder it is widely accepted! The Earthist message, in contrast, seems to consist chiefly in warnings and alarmist predictions to heed which seems to require abandonment of hope by the poor, discomfort of the affluent, and guilt on the part of the rich and powerful. Cassandra may have been right, but she was not popular. Clearly Earthism will not capture the hearts and minds of many people except as it can formulate its message in terms of a convincing hope and a convincing assurance.

That alone will not suffice to win a victory. At most it will position Earthism to triumph when some tragedy of truly horrendous proportions, clearly resulting from economistic practices, strikes the homelands of economism's most powerful supporters. But it is not wrong to hope that these practices can be modified and reversed without such a tragedy.

3 The Marketization of Society

I. THE PLURALISTIC HERITAGE

The victory of nationalism meant the reversal of the relation between the church and the nation. Similarly the victory of economism means first and foremost the reversal of the relation between nation and market, the political and economic spheres. Whereas in nationalism the market serves the nation, in economism, nations are subordinated to the market. The account thus far has emphasized this. But nationalism and economism can both go far beyond this. They often subordinate to themselves other sectors of society as well.

Actually, most nationalisms allowed considerable freedom to various institutions within the society to operate in some independence of government. They were understood to serve the nation best in this way. But within nationalism there are totalitarian tendencies, which usually operate strongly when a nation is at war. These came to expression most systematically in the twentieth century. Nazi Germany, for example, undertook with considerable success to make all sectors of society give up their separate, pluralistic goals and serve the state quite directly in terms of how the Nazi government understood the good of the nation. The educational and legal systems, and even the churches, were expected to aid and abet the purposes of the government even when this required actions contrary to their previously autonomous traditions.

Economism moves in the same totalitarian direction. But this is less noticed because in developed societies it rarely uses physical force or even threats. It accomplishes its goals by convincing people of the truth of its principles and of the gain that will come from applying them. It undercuts the values that have in the past supported relatively autonomous institutions. Step by step it restructures the whole of society around market principles. In the process of becoming a market-driven society, the United States leads the way. To understand this, it is helpful to note some of those sectors of society that

44

have in the past operated on non-market principles and to consider recent changes.

In Christian Europe markets played a secondary role even in the economy. The feudal system dominated agricultural production. The guild system dominated production in the towns and cities. Most prices and wages were set by custom and by judgments of what was fair, rather than by the law of supply and demand. In both systems of production, workers had a direct relation to their products. Especially in the guild system, pride in work was cultivated, and the guilds themselves maintained standards in such a way that neither church nor state had to play much role.

The system of guild production was destroyed by the industrial revolution that took place under nationalism. Industrialization was accompanied by allowing the market to set both prices and wages. Agriculture was not industrialized until the twentieth century, and governments still play a role in setting prices for its products, but the final steps in subordinating agriculture to the market are now being taken.

In Christian Europe there were also professions. These were law, medicine, and ministry. Each was guided by its own ideals, so that practicing a profession meant not only performing particularly skilled work but also operating according to norms established by the profession. The professions were expected to police themselves to ensure that their members adhered to these standards.

Under nationalism the number of professions grew. Teaching, scientific research, engineering, architecture, journalism, and business management are but a few examples of the other fields of work which claimed professional status. The spread of professionalism in part extended the original ethos of professions; in part it dilluted this ethos. For some, a profession became little more than a job for which special training was needed and whose practitioners exercised some control over new membership through a system of accreditation.

The self-governance of the professions meant that the institutions through which they worked had considerable autonomy from one another as well as from any outside force. In the nationalist era, educational, scientific, medical, and legal institutions all had their distinct roles to play and, as long as nationalism did not become totalitarian, all received considerable latitude from the state in playing those roles. For example, the founders of the United States set up a system of checks and balances between the government, on the one side, and, in quite different ways, both legal and religious institutions on the other. This has worked fairly well. None of these institutions had as its primary aim the making of money.

Of course, professionals have always been subject to the temptation to subordinate professional norms to making money. Greed is not an invention of the market system! But the healthy functioning of society has been assumed to depend on the ability of the professions as a whole and the institutions they controlled to subordinate greed to professional ethics.

As recently as fifty years ago it was widely assumed that the primary goal of government was to advance the common good understood in broad social terms. The primary purpose of education had to do with preparing people for a full personal life and for participation and leadership in a democratic society. Scientific research was thought to be guided by the disinterested quest for truth. Law aimed at justice. Health care was geared to benefit patients. Churches and synagogues expressed the ultimate concerns of people and ministered to some of their personal and communal needs. We expected those who served in these ways to be suitably paid, but neither the institutions as a whole, nor those who were employed by them, were thought to be driven by the market mentality.

II. THE MARKETIZATION OF THE PROFESSIONS

Today the situation has changed. All the institutions of society are under pressure to think of themselves and the way they function in market terms. They are also expected to serve the market and are widely evaluated by their success in doing so.

Even in the age of nationalism, governments were concerned with the prosperity of their people. In recent times this prosperity was understood to be furthered by a climate favorable to entrepreneurship and business enterprise. Most governments have been more sensitive to the desires of the rich than to the needs of the poor, partly because elected officials themselves belonged to the upper classes and partly because they needed the support of the rich to win elections. Too often the rich manipulated politics for their own ends. The continuation of these characteristics in our present government is not due to the change from nationalism to economism.

Economism entails the ideological identification of the interests of the market and the major actors in it with the true good of the nation. It has expressed itself in changes in the debate about the income tax. This tax was originally applied only to the rich with the intention of redistributing some of the gains from war profiteering. It was continued as a way of moderating the gap between rich and poor for the sake of the common good. But during the Reagan years the debate changed. The rich, it was argued, were the source of capital investments, whereas the rest of us used our income for current consumption. Since the future well-being of the nation (understood of course in economic terms) depends on investment, income beyond a certain point should be taxed at a lower rate. This economistic interpretation of the role of the income tax was accepted by a Democratic Congress. More recently there was serious discussion of a 'flat tax' that would be applied only to wages and salaries, not to interest and dividends.

Recent 'reforms' have been geared to reducing 'welfare' payments to the poor in order to press them into accepting low-paying jobs in the market. Most of these poor are women with young children. The needs of these children for maternal care receives less consideration than the need to press their mothers into the labor market.

One argument for reducing 'welfare' is the need to cut government expenses so as to balance the budget. It turns out, however, that the first use of these cuts in expenditures is to reduce taxes on capital gains and on inheritance. This additional transfer of income from the poor to the rich is justified as good for the market.

Meanwhile, critics point out that, over and above a continuing Cold War military budget, billions of dollars are devoted to military expenditures not requested by the Pentagon. While the number of military personnel is reduced, procurement continues at a very high volume. Reasons of national security are cited, but the real reason, clearly, is that many businesses profit from these expenditures.

The same reasoning leads to what critics call 'welfare for corporations.' One purpose is to promote their success in selling American products abroad. Since this is good for the American economy, these subsidies are justified in a way that maintaining a floor under the standard of living of the poor is not.

Economistic thinking is moving against government's role in supporting the common good in other ways as well. Typically when governments enact legislation supportive of health, safety, or the environment, some losses are entailed for businesses and property owners. In the past this has been understood as an inevitable part of governance for the common good. But once the good is understood in economistic terms, this appears unjust. The government's basic function is to serve the market. Hence it has no right to take action that distorts the market without compensating those who are injured. Thus far governments have resisted drastic change in this respect, but the tide seems to be turning.

Education is another important field in which market considerations are replacing those that have been primary for millennia. The Greeks understood formal education in terms of *paideia* or the cultivation of human qualities. This kind of education was largely elitist. It was designed primarily for males of the upper classes. The poor were expected to learn trades or engage in unskilled labor. For this purpose even literacy was not required.

The movement toward public education for all developed in the US chiefly out of the need to socialize immigrants from many cultures into the dominant culture and political traditions of the English-speaking nation. Thus it was especially education for American citizenship. This was understood to be humanistically beneficial for the individual, socially beneficial for the nation, and of course economically beneficial for both the individual and the nation.

In recent decades issues of citizenship and personal well-being have faded into the background. The function of public education is increasingly to prepare people for the labor market. Literacy is important because few jobs are available for the functionally illiterate. Increasingly work requires computer literacy as well. It is hoped that schooling will instill disciplines needed for the workplace. In the US arguments for putting more money into public education are characteristically framed in terms of improving the labor force to make the nation more competitive in the global market.

Higher education has a somewhat different history. In the US it was long dominated by liberal arts colleges that carried on something of the paideia tradition. This meant that they had a somewhat elitist character, although this was deeply modified by the democratic context. They functioned for many as a basis of upward mobility. They existed for the purpose of preparing leaders for society. These included the professionals who would maintain the autonomous institutions on which a free society depended. These leaders needed to understand the culture through knowledge of its history. They also needed to assimilate the higher values of that culture and to live by them. This situation predominated until World War II.

Since that war, universities have displaced liberal arts colleges as the main institution of higher education. These universities are composed of a multitude of largely independent units. Increasingly, the great majority of them are designed to prepare people for the better paying jobs in the market. Because the university is the major credentialing agency in society, it has enormous power.

There are still interests and concerns in universities that are not market-driven. Some programs or departments survive even though they are not oriented to getting good jobs for their graduates. But the pressure from students and donors and adminstrators expresses the power of the market. The university as a whole survives and flourishes because of its importance to the market.

Occasionally this becomes completely open and blatant. For example, a 'white paper' issued by the government of the Canadian province of Alberta proposed that the funding of every department of the university be determined by its contribution to the economy of the province. To those whose understanding of education was formed in an earlier era, even more shocking than the attitude of the government was the lack of response from the faculty. Only the chaplains protested the white paper's 'implicit reduction of humanity to servants/tools/commodities of a market economy.'[1]

Much research, whether on university campuses or elsewhere, is also market-driven. The quest for truth has been replaced by the quest to develop marketable products. The great majority of research is paid for by industry or the military. The interest of industry in profits is evident. The relation between military contracts and economistic principles is also real, although a little less direct. The major exception is in the field of health where, alongside market-driven research for pharmaceutical companies, government and foundation money is still available for research not primarily geared to profits.

In extreme instances we are confronted with scientists in the employ of tobacco companies arguing that cigarettes are not addictive and other scientists in the employ of Kuwait or the oil companies arguing that there is no problem of global warming. In asserting the growing dominance of economistic principles in research, it is important not to take these examples as typical. The scientific establishment has not accepted this total prostitution of science to the market.

However, most scientists will do research for which funds are available with little regard to its purposes, and only a small minority insist on pursuing projects aimed at truth that is important for the world even when the market does not support them. So far as research is concerned, 'academic freedom' means chiefly the freedom to sell one's time and skills to the highest bidder. The noble scientific tradition of seeking truth regardless of the cost to the researcher has been marginalized.

The economization or marketization of society is currently being vividly illustrated in the US in the field of medicine. In the past fifty years the public image of the doctor lost much of its luster as the suspicion grew that the doctor's wealth had become as much the goal of medical practice as the patient's health. Nevertheless, considerable confidence remained that on professional grounds doctors *were* committed to the patient's health as well. In one way or another it was assumed that the medical profession would meet urgent needs of anyone regardless of ability to pay. It was also assumed that hospitals would be operated according to professional medical standards.

In the past decade health care has become an 'industry' run for the profit of stockholders and the enrichment of successful CEOs. Patients have become consumers. The industry employs cost-saving techniques that restrict the freedom of doctors to practice as professionals and limit their service to patients. Many find the service they receive from HMOs quite convenient and adequate and are likely to applaud the gains. They are not always aware that some of the 'gains' come from reduced freedom of doctors to do all they might for patients health or from reduced services to the poor. In any case, for good or ill, this represents one more step in ordering the whole of society on market principles.

That lawyers as a whole are highly motivated by the quest for profit is not a recent supposition. One thinks of Dickens' caricature of the legal system in *Bleak House*. The image of lawyers as seeking personal gain more than justice has not been as disturbing as recent suspicion about medical care, because the quest for gain has not seemed as contrary to the professional ethics of lawyers. In the American system lawyers are expected to do their best to win cases for their employers without making judgments as to whether such victories advance the cause of justice or the common good. And, in general, lawyers work for those who pay them best.

The theory of how justice is attained in the American legal system has long had affinities with the market in that it is based on competition between self-interested parties. The parties to the dispute are to present the best cases they can in their own favor. The hope is that the court will be able on this basis to determine what is just. But, as in the market those who are already rich have the advantage in the competition, so also in the courts those who can spend the most money in preparing their case have the advantage. They are in position to employ more, and more skillful, lawyers. To a considerable extent success in the courts is purchased as are other goods available in the market.

These problems are not new. But in an economistic climate, participants in the legal system find maintenance of non-economistic values more difficult. The legal system in capitalist countries has long been accused by Marxists of being little more than a tool of the bourgeoisie in enforcing their control over the proletariat. In fact, the system has often shown itself capable of administering justice even when this worked against the interests of capitalists. The question is whether it can continue to do so in a context in which even the appointment of justices can be strongly influenced by economic actors.

To illustrate the problem of defining justice in a market-driven society, consider the following. In the United States the legal system now incarcerates something like half of its young black men. In the great majority of cases these men have violated the law. In this sense, they are being treated justly on an individual basis. But the cause of so high a percentage of young black men violating the law cannot be understood on individualistic grounds. It has something to do with their collective relation to the economic system. That system generates an underclass and uses the law to protect the other classes from the despair and anger of its members. If the legal system functions increasingly in this way, its administration of 'justice' ceases to be in the service of real justice. It functions instead to support the market.

On the other hand, the ideal of justice continues to play a large role in the legal system in tension with market principles. The state insures that everyone is represented by legal counsel whether they can pay for this or not. Judges and juries are generally concerned that justice be done rather than have money determine the outcome. Many lawyers do *pro bono* work to further this end. The marketization of the legal system is far from complete.

Still, there is currently a growing movement in law schools advocating the employment of economic principles in the law. The leading book for this movement is Richard Posner's *Economic Analysis of the Law*.[2] Leaders of the new movement argue that the 'law's fundamental goal should be to maximize the wealth of society by promoting the efficient use of scarce resources.... They believe the law should mimic the market by seeking only "efficient" legal outcomes, those whose economic benefits outweigh their economic costs.'[3]

During the epoch of Christianism the church cared for the poor. This continued for a long time under nationalism. The industrial revolution, however, created a situation in which it became increasingly necesary for government to take over many functions formerly filled by the church. Primary responsibility for the care of the poor eventually passed into the hands of governments, either local or national.

Just as the church for some time under nationalism maintained its responsibility for the poor; so under economism the state has continued this role. But now economistic thinking is advancing in this area as well. Although there is still great resistance, we seem to be moving toward a situation in which care for the poor will be handled increasingly by the market. It is assumed that when external support is removed, most of the poor will take jobs they now disdain, however poorly they are paid. It is also assumed that the market allows those with resources to use them to relieve the suffering of others when this is their preferred use of these resources. The church will be free to share in this work; so its role will be enlarged along with other voluntary organizations. But for those most fully imbued with the economistic mentality, government should get out of the business of welfare.

The market mentality is affecting the churches as well. When faith is experienced as relating people to a reality transcending all earthly conditions, and when the church functions to nourish and express this experience and its implications, people participate in churches out of deep conviction of the intrinsic importance of doing so. They are likely to select their church on the basis of their perception of the truth or adequacy of its teaching and practice. They may make considerable sacrifices, economic and otherwise, for the sake of their faith. The religious life has little to do with market considerations.

But when the sense of God's reality fades, the church seeks to respond to felt needs of people that do not depend on deep personal conviction. The churches undertake to determine what contributions they can make to the well-being of people which are not better made by other institutions. This can be understood in terms of the churches finding their market niche. This kind of market language can now be found in the rhetoric of the churches themselves.

Obviously, the churches have not been completely marketized. Many decisions are made in an effort to be faithful to their heritage and their God, the consequences of which, in market terms, are not favorable. Many serve the church with no financial recompense and little recognition for their services. Many pastors could do better economically in other professions. Many leave other, more lucrative, jobs in order to minister in the churches.

Nevertheless, if the churches of today are compared with those of fifty or a hundred years ago, the impact of the marketization of society is striking. They must resist if they are to continue to be churches at all. And they are resisting. But resistance becomes ever more difficult.

Effective resistance is possible only as the churches have a basis of knowing what people really need out of their own inherited wisdom. Even this enables them to resist only as, when confronted with this wisdom, people recognize wants and needs they had not heretofore acknowledged. To whatever extent this fails, the survival of the churches depends on their ministering to the felt needs of people who are themselves increasingly socialized into market thinking. Instead of looking for ways of serving God and neighbor, they are likely to be asking whether the church can help them psychologically, socially, or in raising their children. Since offering such help is surely a good thing, the church succumbs to marketing its contributions to meeting these felt needs.

Although the marketization of American society has been part of a worldwide trend, its rapid development in the US has not been accidental. It has been vigorously promoted by moneyed interests. James A. Smith, Executive Director of the Howard Gilman Foundation, summarizes a study that describes the work of conservative, that is, economistically-oriented, foundations. These 'foundations have invested sizable resources to create and sustain an infrastructure of policy, advocacy and training institutions committed to the achievement of conservative policy goals.' They 'directed a majority of their grants to organizations and programs that pursue an overtly ideological agenda based on industrial and environmental deregulation, the privatization of government services, deep reductions in federal anti-poverty spending and the transfer of authority and responsbility for social welfare from the national government to the charitable sector and state and local governments.' Their grantees 'are heavily supported to market policy ideas, cultivate public leadership, lobby policy makers, and build their constituency base.'[4]

The effectiveness of these grants in the marketization of society can be illustrated in relation to the field of law. The rapid growth of the law and economics movement noted above is largely due to gifts of $16.5 million to law schools chiefly to establish chairs in this new field. In addition substantial funds are channelled through George Mason University to its Law and Economics Center 'whose mission is to educated judges in how to apply principles of economic analysis to the law. By 1991, the Center had provided such training...to over 40 percent of the federal judiciary.'[5]

As noted above, the totalitarian tendency of economism, that is, its tendency to shape all aspects of society, operates very differently from the totalitarian state. The changes described above do not involve legal restrictions on behavior. They do not limit freedom of religion, of conscience, of expression, or of assembly. They allow for the maintenance and even extension of democratic elections. They are compatible with a remarkably open society in all these ways. The extension of economistic principles to area after area of society, therefore, does not reduce personal freedom from external coercion. Instead, it is for the sake of increasing the productivity of all workers and, thereby, the total wealth.

III. GLOBAL SOCIETY AS MARKET

One way of understanding the religion of an age is to consider what would constitute its full success. At what does it aim? The ideal aim of Christianity was to order the whole of society to the glory of God as known in Christ. In practice it was to establish and maintain the dominance of the church. That goal became frustrated through the inner division among Christians. For the sake of ideal goals, it became necessary to subordinate the institution that expressed them to the nation state, loyalty to which could be locally unifying.

This locally unifying power drew on linguistic and cultural unity and increasingly on a common history. It was an extension of kinship relations. But whereas Christianity was inherently universalistic, and occasionally tried to realize this universality through the conversion of others and their incorporation into itself, nationalism required difference. It was inherently competitive. The expansion of a nation was usually through domination of others rather than their incorporation. The fulfillment of the national aspirations of France was in conflict with the fulfillment of those of Germany.

In this situation, the ideal or goal could take several forms. One was imperialism, the subordination of other nations to one's own. A second was a balance of power among nations. A third was peaceful and cooperative acceptance of multiple nations. The first and second dominated the affairs of nations through most of their history. The third, as an ideal, was expressed in the League of Nations and subsequently in the UN.

Within the context of nationalism a fourth ideal has emerged. This is the transcendence of nationalism through the transfer of the family feeling embodied in nationalism to wider segments of the human race. For example, some called for Europeanism to replace the strong national feelings of French and Germans. Others wanted to go all the way to an inclusive loyalty to the human race. This can lead to the idealization of world government. Many hoped and expected that a universalistic humanism would succeed nationalism as the operative religion of humanity. But this has not happened.

The economism that has in fact succeeded nationalism is quite different, although it shares the universalism of this ideal. It may even lead to world government, but the government of economism will be quite different from the projection of nationalism onto the global scale. Economism is grounded, not in those aspects of human beings that are informed by differences in beliefs and culture, but in what it takes to be universal, the desire for goods and services. Hence it aims at a world in which all ideological and cultural differences will be subordinated to the common concern to satisfy people's desires as individuals. Such a world is to be a single market in which goods, capital, and perhaps even labor, move freely. In short the global free market is the ideal and goal of economism.

Of course, economism has not existed in pure form free from admixtures of nationalism and even Christianism. Nevertheless, what is remarkable is the clarity of its distinctive vision and its success in the realization of that vision. Noteworthy also is the emergence of global institutions that embody and serve it and their remarkable rise to influence and power.

In broad historical perspective the most important development in the past two decades may prove to be the structural adjustment of the nations of the Third World. This represents economism in almost pure form. The reasons for adjustment are economic. A major purpose is to destroy all nationalistic tendencies in the economies of Third (and now also Second) World countries and merge them into the global market. All social, cultural, educational, medical, and humane considerations, as well as political ones, are subordinated to this goal. Further, the structural adjustment is not forced on these nations by the national power of stronger ones but by economic institutions that are remarkably independent of national ones and are shaped and driven by economistic ideals.

Of course, this is not the first time that many of the peoples of the world have had their economic life dictated to them from without. Colonialism and imperialism had quite similar results in the nationalistic age. But the differences remain striking. Imperialists knew that they were subordinating the interests of the people of the empire to their own. They could do this because of national power, and it was justified by nationalist ideals. Under economism, the beneficiaries are not nations but economic actors, primarily transnational corporations (TNCs). Further, it is sincerely believed that the economic self-interest of economic actors, when fully released from nationalist limitations and other distortions, will fulfill the desires of all people. The adjustments, though they involve surrendering much, are the instruments of salvation. The sacrifice of political power is not to another government but to an impersonal market to which all other nations are to make the same sacrifice.

Even when we recognize that economism is the real religion of our age, we cannot but be surprised at how quickly and dramatically it has conquered nationalism. During the period following World War II, while the institutions of economism were taking shape, far more visible and dramatic was the emergence of new nations, filled with hope and national spirit. Yet within a mere fifty years all that nationalist spirit has been subordinated to the service of the market.

IV. THE INSTITUTIONS OF GLOBAL ECONOMISM

There have always been businesses whose internal principles were economistic. These became powerful and extensive as industrialization advanced during the nationalist period, but they adapted to the social dominance of nationalism. They were clearly located in particular nations and were understood to serve the national interest.

Since World War II, most of the larger corporations have become multinational or, in many cases, transnational. TNCs have become the most important actors in the global market brought into being by the triumph of economism. Indeed, they may have been the most important agents for bringing about this victory.

As their power has become apparent, some of their leaders have come to recognize the responsibility they have for the future of the planet. No more than people generally, do they want to undercut social order or degrade the environment. Their growing concern for the consequences of their actions is a profoundly hopeful sign. Nevertheless, their primary responsibility is to their stockholders rather than to humanity generally. If socially and environmentally favorable policies would render them uncompetitive, they cannot afford to adopt them.

TNCs did not achieve this dominance by their own actions alone. The primary direct agents in the change have been national governments themselves. Some of the support for policies favorable to corporations has been because political leaders are beholden to persons of wealth who profit from the shift to the global market, but much of it has also been due to conversion to economistic thinking. In any case, in recent years governments have transferred power to TNCs through deregulation and reduced corporate taxes as well as direct subsidy and support. Especially important is their renunciation of the use of national boundaries to maintain national economies through tariffs and quotas.

This sacrifice of national power to TNCs did not come about abruptly or easily. It required the sustained work of many committed persons. One expression of this commitment was the Trilateral Commission. This has recently been demonized as a secret conspiracy threatening to national interests. It was not secret, and it was a conspiracy only in the sense in which any cooperative work among people with shared convictions about the changes they want to see implemented can be called conspiratorial. But it *was* threatening to national interests in the sense that it aimed to subordinate nationalistic interests to the common good understood in economistic terms. That means that the direct beneficiaries here, as in most cases of the application of global economism, have been the TNCs. The Trilateral Commission expressed, therefore, the idealism of the new religion struggling against the continuing power of the old.

How influential it has been is a matter of dispute. Since it included many of the opinion-makers and policy-shapers of the world, its influence should not be underestimated. The goals at which it aimed are being realized. Whether this would have happened without its work, or happened as rapidly, cannot be known.

In addition to such unofficial organizations, there have been official ones. One of the most important has been GATT, which came into being shortly after World War II and has worked in a sustained way to reduce trariffs and other barriers to trade in this post-war period. Its greatest success was the Uruguay Round which established the WTO. WTO has enormous power for the settlement of trade disputes between nations and between corporations and nations.

Whereas nations, especially the US, have been unwilling to transfer power to international organizations such as the UN or the World Court, they are willing signatories of the Uruguay Round of GATT. This means that they are prepared to allow WTO, in some cases, to overrule national and state legislation that is deemed to restrain trade. As the market assumes a more and more dominant role in society, transnational organizations that can set aside national legislation for the sake of globalizing the market have the makings of a kind of world government. MAI will further this transnational control of the internal life of nations.

It may be that as the full power of such economistic institutions is appreciated, they will come to take more responsibility for their actions in terms of their social and environmental consequences. But this is a hope that is not based on current events. Thus far legislation directed to social and environmental concerns is threatened rather than supported by the WTO's stated purpose of enhancing trade.

Although all of these institutions of economism deserve study, this book deals primarily with the BWI – the IMF and

the World Bank. These were established in an early foreshadow-
ing of the economistic spirit in the waning months of World
War II. Their stated purposes expressed that spirit, and it has
been nurtured within them. They rose gradually to positions
of great influence, bursting on the scene in the eighties as the
most powerful global instruments for the implementation of
the new religious faith.

Of these two, the Bank will be the focus of attention. The
task of the IMF has been narrowly economistic, and it has
given little attention to other considerations. The Bank, on the
other hand, was established officially as the International
Bank for Reconstruction and Development (IBRD). Although
the goals of reconstruction and development were understood in economistic ways, the effort to fulfil its purposes has
led it into broader humanistic and environmental considerations. These have played a much larger role in the Bank than
in any other institution of global economism. The question is
whether this role can become so large that the Bank can lead
the world beyond economism to Earthism. The following five
chapters are chiefly a study of the Bank with this question in
mind.

NOTES

1. 'Gov't Paper Fosters Reprehensible Values,' *Edmonton Journal*, 11 May
    1994.
2. Richard Posner, *The Economic Analysis of the Law*. Boston: Little, Brown,
    1977.
3. Alliance for Justice, *Justice for Sale: Shortchanging the Public Interest for
    Private Gain*. Washington: Alliance for Justice, 1993, p. 24.
4. Sally Covington, *Moving a Public Policy Agenda: The Strategic Philanthropy
    of Conservative Foundations*. Washington: National Committee for
    Responsive Philanthropy, July 1997, p. 1.
5. Ibid., p. 9.

4 The Bretton Woods Institutions

I. BRETTON WOODS

The economistic age was ushered in at Bretton Woods, New Hampshire, in 1944. While most of the world's attention was directed to the establishment of the United Nations, the actions taken at Bretton Woods would prove, in the long run, more fateful. These actions were about the organization of the global economic order.

At the time, and for some years thereafter, the great importance of the work of Bretton Woods was not apparent. It seemed technical and narrowly focused in a world whose problems were enormous and basic. Bretton Woods was only tangentially concerned with recovery from the vast destruction caused by World War II. Its emphasis was on the more distant future, on what would happen after normalcy had returned.

Nevertheless, there was at Bretton Woods a sense of inaugurating something new, something of sacred worth. In his speech moving to accept the Final Act, John Maynard Keynes marveled that representatives of 44 nations had worked together so well. He concluded: 'If we can so continue, this nightmare in which most of us here present have spent too much of our lives will be over. The brotherhood of man will have become more than a phrase.'[1] Keynes' special interest was in the World Bank. He 'never ceased to claim that this unprecedented Bank could do no less than help to remake the world in a finer image and contribute to the brotherhood of man.'[2]

That the goal of Bretton Woods was to introduce a new age in which the mistakes of the old would not recur was clear in the speech of US Treasury Secretary, Henry Morgenthau. 'All of us have seen the great economic tragedy of our time. We saw the worldwide depression of the 1930s. We saw currency disorders develop and spread from land to land, destroying the basis for international trade and international investment and even international faith. In their wake, we saw unemployment and wretchedness – idle tools, wasted wealth. We saw their victims fall prey, in places, to demagogues and dictators. We saw bewilderment and bitterness become the breeders of fascism, and, finally, of war.'[3] The BWI were to ensure that nothing like that would happen again.

What is noteworthy is that the institutions that were to save the world from such horrors were to be purely economic ones. Of course, others were looking for such salvation in a political institution for international cooperation. But here at Bretton Woods were gathered those who were certain that the real problems were economic and that a technical economic approach would solve them. This is the economistic mindset that was eventually to dominate the post-World War II scene. At Bretton Woods it was engaged in creating the economistic institutions that would be the instruments of salvation.

The view that the war was at least partly caused by the depression was widely shared. Morgenthau's view that currency disorders played a large causal role in the depression was also common. Even if these did not by themselves cause the depression, it was and is widely believed that the actions of nations in devaluing their currencies prolonged and deepened what might otherwise have been a modest depression, so that it became a world-historical event that will long be remembered as The Depression.

Because of this perception of events, economists within the United States from an early point in the war years began thinking about how to avoid the recurrence of such a depression. They assumed that there would continue to be recessions from time to time, but they believed that trade among nations could be managed so that it would be a mitigating, instead of an aggravating, force. Discussions about how this could be done were initiated in the Department of the Treasury. Already in April, 1942, Harry White, the assistant secretary, wrote a 'Proposal for a United Nations Stabilization Fund and a Bank for Reconstruction and Development of the United and Associated Nations.'

This proposal became the basis for extensive discussion in the US government and between the US and Great Britain and Canada. Detailed discussion dealt chiefly with what White called the International Stabilization Fund (ISF). He defended this strongly against John Maynard Keynes' proposal of an International Clearing Union. Chiefly because of the relative weakness of Great Britain at the time, Keynes was forced to yield, although some of the goals of his plan were integrated into that of White.

The basic purpose of the ISF would be to insure that international trade would not be disrupted by temporary problems in the balance of trade or shortages of the necessary currency. It assumed trading patterns among nations at more or less the same stage of development. Here the situation could arise that nation A wants to buy from nation B but does not have sufficient currency of that nation to pay. The ISF would provide the necessary currency to keep trade moving smoothly in exchange for the currency of nation A.

The assumption is that nation A has a basically healthy economy, that its shortage of the requisite currency is temporary. If nation A continues to purchase the currency of other nations and shows no signs of being able to sell it back, the ISF would have to set conditions for further purchases that would insure that the balance of trade would be adjusted. This was called conditionality, and this power became the basis for the massive conditions imposed on debtor nations in more recent times. There was no intention to finance long-term deficits.

The fund would be established by contributions from all the member countries. The amounts of other currencies they could purchase would be tied to the amount of their own initial contribution. The idea was that nations would need to use this fund in some ratio to the size of their economy and the volume of their trade.

A second feature of the Fund would be that its members not be allowed to discriminate in their policies. This was directed especially against the prewar trading policies among the British Commonwealth nations. Americans had been largely excluded from these markets because American goods had to overcome trading barriers that did not exist within the commonwealth system. The principle of nondiscrimination did not mean that trade had to be free from tariffs or other restrictions, only that these must be imposed equally on all participating states.

A third feature had to do with currency restrictions. These were to be liberalized. The goal would be that currency for international trade would not be controlled or restricted. This did not mean that there was any objection to control over capital transfers. Indeed, these were expected.

A fourth goal was to stabilize currencies. Trade is easier if the relative value of the currencies of the countries involved remains the same. Trade is especially disrupted when countries arbitrarily devalue their currencies so as to make their goods cheaper in other countries or raise their value so as to make purchases easier. The ISF was to work for stable exchange rates. These were to be pegged to the US dollar which, in turn, was pegged to gold.

Those who proposed this institution and these functions recognized that the ISF could not realize its goals immediately. In the process of recovering from the war, nations could not immediately effect these policies. Hence, built into the proposal was a period of transition.

By the time of Bretton Woods the US, Great Britain, and Canada had come to agreement on most of the plan, now called the International Monetary Fund (IMF). Only a few features were genuinely open for contributions by the delegates from the other 41 countries, including the Soviet Union. Virtually all the amendments they proposed were rejected. The overwhelming economic power of the US was recognized, and the other nations were willing to accept its leadership.

The IMF (together with the World Bank) came into existence when the Bretton Woods accords were ratified in Savannah, Georgia, in 1946. By that time the Soviet Union had dropped out, planning to go it alone rather than to accept the conditions of international trade imposed by the US. Since the period of transition in which its policies could not be fully implemented lasted for many years, the IMF was a relatively obscure institution for some time. One of the participants in its creation comments in retrospect, 'the Fund remained largely irrelevant for the first fifteen years of its existence.'[4]

This judgment is exaggerated. Although the Fund was geared to the period after reconstruction had taken place, it did help for 25 years to maintain relatively stable exchange rates. This was a major part of its mission. It also loaned money on a short-term basis, as planned, to facilitate international trade. Some of these loans involved 'conditionalities,' that is, they required recipients to take steps that would insure a return to balance in their international accounts. These loans were made almost entirely to industrial nations, since the claims on its funds of Third World nations were very small. All of this took place smoothly and inconspicuously. The IMF was not a highly visible actor on the world scene during that period.

The relative strength of the US was at its peak at the time of Bretton Woods and during the years immediately thereafter. With the recovery of Europe and Japan its relative economic standing declined. The heavy costs of the Vietnam War in the 1960s drained its resources and led to large holdings of dollars in other hands. Confidence in the value of the dollar declined, and this resulted in greater demands for the gold to which it was pegged.

The solution adopted by the US was to de-link the dollar from gold and to devalue it. This fundamentally reversed the policies on which the IMF was based. It ended the possibility of maintaining stable exchange rates by pegging all currencies to the dollar. Hence a large part of the mandate of the Fund was undercut. Liquidity was attained with little application for loans from the IMF. In the words of Robert S. Browne, by the mid-seventies 'the IMF was a large and well-paid bureaucracy with very little to do.'[5]

During that period most disruptions occurred in the Third World. The IMF became involved with Third World nations that were having difficulty with debt payments. In response to their need it helped in the renegotiating of debt payments and offered stabilization loans to assist countries in making the changes necessary to insure payments. But up until 1982 the world-historical importance of this activity was not apparent.

II. THE WORLD BANK

Prior to Bretton Woods much less thought went into the World Bank. Although White had included such a bank in his initial proposal, the American discussion had concentrated on the Fund. This left an opening for the British, and it was Keynes who brought a proposal to the Americans. It was this proposal, modified in debate, that was discussed at Bretton

Woods. Since Keynes also chaired the section in which it was discussed, he has primary responsibility for the formation of the World Bank.

Whereas the function of the IMF was to keep trade moving smoothly and in a balanced way, the Bank was to assist with reconstruction after the war by making long-term project loans primarily to governments. In this sense, Bretton Woods was dealing with an immediate problem. On the other hand, for the Bank to be the major instrument for reconstruction, it would have had to be much larger and have greater flexibility.

As it was, although Great Britain's needs were great, Keynes did not expect that Britain would borrow from the Bank. He worked out a separate loan from the United States. That loan, $3.75 billion dollars, was considerably more than the $3.175 billion US contribution to the capitalization of the Bank, and of the latter, only 20 percent was to be paid in. Further, the loan to Britain was only the beginning of US lending for the reconstruction of Europe.

Contrary to expectation, there was little demand for World Bank loans. These were to be made only under the conditions of the fiscal worthiness of the borrower. Also they were not to compete with commercial loans. These conditions were rarely met. The Bank needed to act conservatively in order to establish its own credit-worthiness with Wall Street, because most of the money it would lend would be borrowed on the capital markets. In the chaotic conditions of post-war Europe, its lending requirements were too stringent. The needed funds were provided instead by the Marshall Plan. By 1953 the Bank had made total loans of just $1.75 billion, whereas the Marshall Plan had transferred $41.3 billion.[6] In short, the Bank was not a major player.

The Bank began to focus on the second part of its mission – development. Here, too, it was not confronted with loan requests that met its requirements in anything like the amounts it was prepared to lend. It was not to make loans which the private sector was ready to undertake. On the other hand, it was expected to make loans that were good and reliable investments. It found that it could not wait for requests to come to it. It must, instead, take the initiative in working with developing countries to help them plan projects that were fundable.

This was not easy. In many instances the Bank had to set up agencies, in some independence of governments, that specialized in working with them in planning large scale projects suitable for Bank funding. EGAT in Thailand and NTPC in India are typical examples.[7] It favored projects in energy generation and transportation in the belief that as the infrastructure developed, workers would become more productive and the whole economy would improve.

Although World Bank lending prior to 1970 was a minor factor in the total capital flow to developing nations, the Bank already had disproportionate influence in shaping development policies. It brought together development workers from different agencies to coordinate their efforts, and it established training programs for indigenous leaders. Thus it played a major role in conceptualizing development and in giving it direction.

Of the many questions to be raised about this whole process, one of the most interesting is the relation of the Bank to governments and politics. It was established as an economistic institution. This label is justified first by the fact that both White and Keynes wanted it to work on technical economic grounds. They thought it could promote ecomomic growth without being involved in politics. This was written into its charter, so that it was to work in countries of all political types and not to interfere.

The assumption was that the economic order can be sharply distinguished from the political one. During the long regime of Eugene Black, 1949–63, there was a serious effort to keep aloof from other than technically economic matters. But even then, the boundary could not be perfect. He acknowledged that 'we have made no secret of the fact that we sometimes refuse to lend to countries which are pursuing unsound policies or to borrowers who, because of governmental restrictions on rates, are unable to maintain a sound financial position ... When we lend we want our money to contribute to the growth of local savings and to stimulate their application to productive purposes. We do not think it is the Bank's role to help governments postpone the difficult decisions needed to mobilize local resources.'[8]

Perhaps more influential in broadening the Bank's work beyond narrowly economic issues was the initiation of country missions in 1949. These were sent by the Bank in response to requests for advice and counsel. The advice was focused on economic issues, but these could not be separated from broader policy. 'In the late 1950s such missions frequently preceded independence and Bank membership for former colonies; they were significant in the start of an operational relationship, especially in many African countries with a poor planning base.'[9] Clearly, insofar as the Bank committed itself to economic development, it could not avoid influencing the policies of the countries with which it worked.

The Bank has been an economistic institution also in that through most of its history it has been relatively free from external governmental control. Keynes wanted it to be run by its own bureaucracy with little influence from governments. The US insisted that its governing board consist of representatives of member governments. In the beginning this board took its duties seriously. This resulted in a clash with its first president, Eugene Mayer, and his resignation after only one year. After that, however, the decisions were largely left to the president and his staff. The governmental representatives have played a rather minor role. They must approve the Bank's projects, and they are free to seek information in earlier stages, but as a rule they learn about them only at the end. Their role is only rarely more than rubber-stamping what has already been agreed upon. In this respect the Bank has been remarkably a-political.

This could easily be exaggerated. Changes of basic Bank policy require Board approval. Also, the president is always an American selected by the government of the United States, and the Bank can be viewed cynically as an agency of the US government. In fact, however, the US has little direct involvement in its internal policy-formation and decision-making.

The independence of the Bank is fostered by the fact that once it received its initial capitalization and established good credit with the international financial markets, it has been largely independent financially. Only occasionally does it return to its member governments for support. This means that it has little need for the approval of its member nations. It is largely self-governing and self-perpetuating.

This is most striking in its relation to the UN. Although its establishment was prior to the UN, officially it belongs to that body and should be governed by policies established by the General Assembly. However, already in 1947, it secured an agreement that rendered it virtually autonomous. It does not need to share its information with the UN, and since it can describe UN policies as political and assert its own nonpolitical character, it is free to ignore the General Assembly's wishes.

Thus the World Bank is an autonomous economic institution. Since its founders believed that by working only in the area of economics the Bank could solve many problems, I have called it economistic. But the fullest embodiment of economism requires another step. Economism aims at a situation in which the political sphere (and, increasingly, others as well) is subordinated to the economic. In due course the work of the Bank came to illustrate this as well.

Once a developing country began to work with the Bank, its internal political life was altered. The Bank favored some of its leaders over others and supported some of its institutions more than others. As noted above, it even created new quasi-governmental agencies that then had enormous influence because of their economic power. By organizing the total development effort, it influenced all sectors of society. Thus even in the period before 1970, when the political role of the Bank was not so obvious, the groundwork was well laid. Developing countries were learning the political importance of working with the Bank. Precisely by claiming to be technically economic, and therefore apolitical, the Bank took on an extremely important political role. It encouraged the subordination of social, cultural, and political values to economic ones.

Development as conventionally understood did take place quite rapidly during the period we are considering. Global economic growth averaged five percent a year, leading to a tripling of the world economy. This growth seemed to be led by the unprecedented increase in world trade. During the sixties the rate of growth of developing countries reached 6 percent a year.[10] Although it is not possible to sort out the Bank's role from the many other factors contributing to this growth, the Bank could legitimately claim some success.

Still, there were reasons to be troubled. To some extent the growth in the developing countries was a function of capital transfer to them. Now there was danger that this transfer would cease. Repayment of loans was at times greater than the volume of new loans, and there were indications that this situation would intensify. This is an entirely foreseeable situation, and it would not be troubling in most contexts. But a net transfer of capital from the developing world to the North threatened to stop the development to which the Bank was committed.

A World Bank report in 1969[11] pointed out that by 1967 Latin American borrowers had to devote seven-eighths of their new loans to servicing their debts, and that within a few years all their loans would be required for this purpose. Under these circumstances, to whatever extent borrowing had fueled development, development would be slowed.

There were other reasons to be troubled. One of the goals of the Bank was to alleviate poverty and reduce the gap between rich and poor. Many economists believe that sufficient economic growth accomplishes this by itself. Hence most development projects had been directed toward overall growth. However, overall growth had left large segments of the society behind, relatively, and perhaps absolutely, worse off than before.

The UN provided a forum in which the concerns of Third World people could be heard. In December of 1970 the Assembly resolved '(a) to leave no sector of the population outside the scope of change and development; (b) to effect structural change which favors national development and to activate all sectors of the population to participate in the development process; (c) to aim at social equality, including the achievement of an equitable distribution of income and wealth in the nation; (d) to give high priority to the development of the human potential including vocational and technical training, and the provision of employment opportunities and meeting the needs of the children.'[12]

These aims include the economic ones but are much broader. The Bank certainly did not oppose them. But for the most part Bank loans were not geared to attaining them except on the assumption that overall economic growth would in itself lead to meeting all these goals. Although the Bank was not obligated to follow the lead of the UN Assembly, the concerns of the Assembly did resonate with some leaders in the Bank.

III. BLACK'S ADDITIONS

The World Bank was established to work with national governments. It could lend money only to governments. Yet its leaders realized that much of the needed development would occur only through private investment and initiative. Indeed, purely economistic thinking favored private investment over public.

For fourteen years from 1949 to 1963 Eugene Black was president of the Bank. One of his major goals was to break the restriction with regard to working with private corporations. To this end it was necessary to have a separate organization with a different charter. One of Black's major accomplishments was the establishment of an affiliate, the International Finance Corporation (IFC), an institution 'for tackling the problems of private investors generally and promoting their activities.'[13]

The IFC is part of the World Bank family, coming under the World Bank president. Accordingly, the term World Bank has become ambiguous. Often it refers to the whole World Bank family. When the original institution is to be distinguished from the IFC and later additions, it is best to speak of the IBRD. However, through the following chapters, references to the Bank will have IBRD primarily in view.

The IFC works with the private sector. It provides information about investment opportunities. It lends money for projects itself but also seeks private parties to share in financing these projects. Because its primary mission is to increase involvement of the private sector in investments, the interest in the broader aims of development that have played an increasing role in the IBRD have been much less pronounced in the IFC.

The relative importance of the IBRD and the IFC has varied under Black's successors. George Woods, who followed him as president, strongly supported the IFC and transferred to it whatever projects he could. While McNamara continued to affirm the need for TNC investments in the developing nations, he brought back to the IBRD some of the programs Woods had turned over to the IFC. The great expansion that occurred under his leadership was chiefly in the Bank's own program of lending. But under his successor, Alden W.

Clausen, the Bank's emphasis again shifted to support for private investment.

As the great importance of private investment became apparent, the Bank established two other agencies to further this. One problem for investors was the difficulty of resolving disputes with host countries. Their laws varied greatly, and investors were not always confident of being treated fairly. In 1965 the Bank created the International Center for Settlement of Investment Disputes (ICSID). Its function is one of conciliation and arbitration. When disputes are submitted to it by private companies and national governments, each appoints a member to the panel that will hear the arguments and these two agree upon a third.

Another major reason for hesitating to invest in a developing country has been fear that changes in governmental policy will undercut agreements. Investors especially fear nationalization of their companies, but there are many other legislative changes that can affect them adversely. There are also risks to investments due to political unrest or civil war. To remove this obstacle to investment, the bank established the Multilateral Investment Guarantee Agency (MIGA) in 1988. This works closely with the IFC.

Despite enthusiastic support for private investment, until recently IFC and its allied institutions were secondary players in the work of the Bank. This situation is now changing. In the 90s TNC investments in the Third World have come greatly to surpass those of the Bank itself. Working with private investors has become a major part of the Bank's function. There is likelihood that the affiliates established for this purpose by the Bank will become its dominant force.

Black was concerned about another type of limitation on the Bank's work as well. The Bank was chartered to be a fiscally responsible organization. It was expected to make money on its development loans. The theory was that good investments by national governments would be profitable, so that the government could repay the loan with interest and still come out ahead.

Black recognized that there were countries so poor that they needed more generous help. This help would still take the form of loans, but these loans would be at very low interest rates. They would not be repaid rapidly enough for there to be adequate funds for future loans.

Whereas the Bank could borrow money on the international financial markets for most of its lending, it could not do so for these. First World governments would have to provide the funds, and they would need to be expended through a separate agency. Accordingly, he created the International Development Agency (IDA) to enable the Bank to deal more generously with its poorest clients.

Since IDA, like IBRD, loans to governments rather than private corporations, these two are closely linked. Hence the Bank family can be understood loosely as composed of two parts: IBRD and IDA, on the one side, and IFC, ICSID, and MIGA, on the other. The following chapters will deal primarily with the former.

NOTES

1. Susan George and Fabrizio Sabelli, *Faith and Credit: The World Bank's Secular Empire*. Boulder: Westview Press, 1994, p. 34.
2. Ibid., p. 35.
3. Ibid., p. 27.
4. Raymond F. Mikesell, *The Bretton Woods Debates: A Memoir*, 'Essays in International Finance,' No. 192. Princeton: International Finance Section, Department of Economics, Princeton University, March 1994, p. 60.
5. Robert S. Browne, 'Alternatives to the International Monetary Fund,' in John Cavanagh, Daphne Wysham, and Marcos Arruda, eds, *Beyond Bretton Woods: Alternatives to the Gobal Economic Order*. London and Boulder: Pluto Press with Institute for Policy Studies and Transnational Institute, 1994, p. 60.
6. Bruce Rich, *Mortgaging the Earth: The World Bank, Environmental Impoverishment, and the Crisis of Development*. Boston: Beacon Press, 1994, p. 68.
7. Rich, op. cit., p. 74.
8. 'Comments of President Eugene Black on discussion of Annual Report, IBRD,' *Summary of Proceedings, Eleventh Annual Meeting of the Board of Governors, Washington, D.C., September 24–28, 1956*. Washington: World Bank, 15 November 1956, p. 13. See Jochen Kraske, et al., *Bankers with a Mission: The Presidents of the World Bank, 1946–1991*. Oxford: Oxford University Press, 1996, p. 91.
9. Kraske, op. cit., p. 90.
10. Advisory Group on Economic Matters, WCC/CCPD, *International Financial System: An Ecumenical Challenge*. Geneva: World Council of Churches, 1985, p. 20.

11.   The Pearson Commission Report, *Partners in Development*. See Morris
      Miller, *Coping Is Not Enough: The International Debt Crisis and the Roles
      of the World Bank and International Monetary Fund*. Homewood, IL:
      Dow Jones-Irwin, 1986, p. 49.
12.   UN General Assembly Resolution No. 2681. Wilfred L. David, *The
      IMF Policy Paradigm*. New York: Praeger Publishers, 1985, p. 112.
13.   Kraske, op. cit., p. 105.

5 The McNamara Years

I. McNAMARA'S POLICIES

In 1968 Robert McNamara had become president of the Bank. He remained so until 1981. During that period the Bank was transformed from being one of many significant actors in the development of the Third World to dominating the field. Also, it shed its reluctance to deal directly with the inner life of countries and to press its agenda upon them. McNamara understood that economic development could not be separated from social, cultural, and political development.

The change can be seen first in the volume of loans. In constant dollars these increased six-fold. During his first five-year term, the Bank financed more projects and loaned more money than in all of its previous 22-year history. This was McNamara's response to the danger that the capital flow to the South would end or even reverse itself. As long as the volume of new loans increased sufficiently, the portion of the new loans needed to repay the old ones would remain low! Further, McNamara believed that with a sufficient inflow of funds, the economy of a developing country would grow. Hence it was more important that projects be approved than exactly what they were.

This conviction had enormous consequences. Pressure to increase the volume of loans led to rewarding employees less according to the care with which they developed projects and the success ulitmately achieved. The Bank began to reward employees more according to the quantity of money they succeeded in loaning. Since the loans were to governments and the Bank was to be paid before any other creditor, their security did not depend on the economic value of the project. The Bank would be repaid in any case. Meanwhile, according to McNamara's thinking, the money would stimulate the economy of the recipient country even if it was not spent well.

Although overall growth in the economy remained the major way the Bank under McNamara undertook to deal with world poverty, he led it also to target many of its projects specifically to the sectors in society that had failed to participate in development. He estimated that nine hundred million people 'subsist on incomes of less that $75 a year in an environment of squalor, hunger, and hopelessness. They are the absolute poor, living in situations so deprived as to be below any rational definition of human decency.'[1]

McNamara emphasized that this condition of poverty had not been reduced by the general increase in per capita income in developing countries. In direct contradiction to the standard economistic view that economic growth is the means of dealing with poverty, he stated: 'But what is most misleading of all is to assume that once we have calculated the GNP growth rate of a particular developing country, and then expressed it in per capita terms, we have arrived at a sound picture of the level of economic development in the country.... For rates of growth of GNP, and of GNP per capita, tell us nothing about how income is actually distributed within a country.'[2] If the Bank's practice over the years, or even during McNamara's tenure, had been fully informed by this understanding, many of the problems with its work would not have occurred. For McNamara, his correct statement implied only that in addition to efforts to increase the GNP, the Bank must target some programs directly to help the poor.

The Bank did devote a rapidly growing portion of its loans to projects for the poor. Some of these were for improving conditions in urban slums. More were directed to peasant farmers. McNamara's goal was that production on small farms throughout the developing world would, by 1985, increase at an annual rate of 5 percent. By 1981 31 percent of the Bank's new loans were being made for rural development.

In some respects McNamara's policies carried economism further than ever. The Bank as an economic institution unabashedly undertook to reshape societies all over the world. In another respect, however, McNamara qualified economism. He decided that trusting overall economic growth to take care of the problem of poverty was not satisfactory. He shaped Bank policies out of compassion for the poorest of the poor and for the sake of justice. There is no reason to doubt his sincerity in this respect.

The theoretical shift here is important. Economism always presents itself as the way to solve human problems, and especially that of poverty. In its purest form, however, the solution is by economic growth alone. In the economistic view, the appropriate policies are those that generate the most sustained and rapid growth. Poverty alleviation is expected to take care of itself in that context. As long as the lot of the poor is improved, the spread between rich and poor is not important. Hence, direct efforts to help the poor are not needed or desirable.

McNamara disagreed with economistic thinking on this point. Appealing to the teachings of traditional religions, he wrote: 'The extremes of privilege and deprivation are simply no longer acceptable.'[3] Reducing the spread by favoring the poor over the rich was for McNamara a distinct and important goal of Bank activity. The argument of Hollis Chenery in *Redistribution with Growth*[4] that 'income redistribution could take place without slowing developing nations' rates of growth...became...the Bank's intellectual centerpiece in its marching order through the 1970s.'[5]

It could, indeed, be argued that targeting the poor is an effective strategy for generating sustained growth. This was McNamara's claim. For him there was no tension between focusing on projects in rural development and aiming at the overall growth of the economy. Targeting poverty was one way of accomplishing the latter task.[6] Still, it was a better way for moral reasons. In McNamara's Bank, moral considerations played a role not to be expected in a purely economistic institution.

Before McNamara the Bank was already encouraging coherent development planning in Third World nations. McNamara undertook to advance this work. In 1970 he announced his plan for 'a new and expanded program of Country Economic Missions' whose purpose it would be 'to assist the member government to draw up an overall development strategy which will include every major sector of the economy, and every relevant aspect of the nation's social framework.'[7] Granted, the operative verb was 'to assist,' but the end for which the assistance was to be offered involved changing 'every relevant aspect of the nation's social framework.' There was no longer any idea that economic development could be carried on without intervening in other spheres of a nation's life.

McNamara brought to the World Bank great concern about population issues. In his view 'short of thermonuclear war itself, it is the gravest issue the world faces over the decades immediately ahead.'[8] By far the fastest growth is in the Third World, and McNamara was convinced that 'it is the population explosion which, by holding back the advancement of the poor, is blowing apart the rich and the poor and widening the already dangerous gap between them.'[9] He called for informing developing nations about the problem, financing family planning programs, and advancing research. Although McNamara's keen analysis and strong rhetoric have disappeared from World Bank statements, it has continued programs in this field – $200 million in 1994.[10]

Although tying the population issue to economic ones reflects the basic economistic character of the Bank, McNamara's approach to this problem was not basically economistic. The economistic approach to population growth expressed itself in the doctrine of the population transition. Based on the experience of the West, this held that in developed societies when economic growth had brought about a certain level of prosperity, people chose to have fewer children, and population leveled off. The implication was that in developing societies all attention should be directed to economic growth and that success in that field would take care of the problem of excessive population growth. This is analogous to the economistic view that economic growth will overcome poverty without special attention to the causes of poverty.

McNamara recognized that these economistic doctrines are erroneous. The causes of poverty other than the size of the overall economy must be analyzed and addessed in their own terms. Population issues also must be considered independently. The Bank has accepted these judgments and acted on them with varying degrees of commitment to the present time.

1970 represents a convenient date to view the change in the Bank in relation to environmental issues. It is the year of the first Earth Day, a time of the awakening of the world to the environmental devastation that was associated with economic growth. Since the Bank had long been involved in promoting growth, its own projects could be seen in retrospect as among the most destructive.

McNamara was quick to respond by employing James A. Lee as environmental advisor. After several bureaucratic permutations, Lee became head of the Office of Environmental and Scientific Affairs. At the UN Conference on the Human Environment at Stockholm in 1972 McNamara asserted: 'The question is not whether there should be continued economic growth. There must be. Nor is the question whether the impact on the environment must be respected. It has to be. Nor – least of all – is it a question of whether these two considerations are interlocked. They are. The solution of the dilemma revolves clearly not about whether, but how.'[11] McNamara assured the conference that 'in cooperation with other development agencies, we have designed a careful set of guidelines, and have built into our whole economic assistance strategy a feasible method for correlating ecological protection with effective and cost-conscious development. What we have discovered is significant. By careful analysis, we have found, in every instance to date, that we can reduce the danger of environmental hazards either at no cost to the project, or at a cost so moderate that the borrower has been fully agreeable to accepting the necessary safeguards.'[12]

II. AN EVALUATION

Unfortunately, the course of history in the seventies did not realize McNamara's intentions. This was partly because of events over which the Bank had no control. But it was also partly the direct result of the Bank's actions.

Despite many excellent initiatives on the part of the Bank, the gap between rich and poor continued to grow. The growing gap could be traced in part to the continued dominance of the Bank's characteristic preference for large projects aimed at infrastructure development which had always benefited the rich more directly than the poor. For example, the huge dams favored by the World Bank always displaced the people who lived in the flooded areas, and, despite good intentions, few of these people were satisfactorily resettled. Development of 'undeveloped' areas such as tropical forests displaces indigenous people, and few of these adjust well to the new situations into which they are thrust.

It would be unfair and misleading to speak of McNamara's efforts to help the poor only in terms of failures. David Beckman, who worked on some of these projects, reports that several 'were top down failures. But other projects benefited hundreds of thousands of low-income families. In La Paz, Bolivia, for example, tens of thousands of slum dwellers received title to their land and basic services, partly because the World Bank was on their side.'[13]

Regrettably, the Bank's own studies showed that its rural development projects frequently benefited the bureaucracy and the landlords while bypassing the poorer peasants, increased the number of the landless, and worsened their condition. Increasing production usually meant modernization, which substituted oil-based inputs for solar energy and human labor.

The Green Revolution was fostered by the World Bank with the best intentions and with great success in increasing yields. Yet a review of its effects in a conference in Puerto Rico in 1979 concluded that it 'failed to significantly improve the condition of the poor. . . . "Green Revolution" technology was not developed with the poor in mind . . . The decision to promote new agricultural technologies that are beyond the means of the poor dislocated the rural people from their lands and engendered a new poverty.'[14]

The Bank drew the conclusion from its failures, not that top-down development is inherently distorting, but that the societies it was seeking to help misused the aid. This misuse, it decided, was based on structural factors in these societies that led to inefficient use of resources. McNamara decided that without structural adjustment, general prosperity would never be attained. Hence, in 1980 the Bank began making structural adjustment a condition for some of its loans. It also began making loans geared to assisting in such structural adjustment. Turkey was the first recipient. In this instance the adjustments were largely initiated by Turkey and supported by the BWI.[15] The ordering of all of society to economic ends took an additional step.

The close working of the Bank with governments in planning development for all sectors of society had led, not to support of democratic movements, but to alliances with authoritarian governments. Indeed, having moved from ignoring the nature of governments to becoming involved with all dimensions of society, the Bank refused loans to democratically-elected governments in Chile and Brazil and worked closely with the military leaders who overthrew them. The Bank was also unusually generous to Rumania when if became a member, despite or because of the concentrated authority exercised by Ceaucescu.

None of this should lead to questioning McNamara's sincerity, or that of those who followed him. It seems, instead, to be a virtually inevitable outcome of vigorous pursuit of the goal of economic growth by a centralized economistic institution. The economic analysis of need concentrates on macro-economic factors rather than on political or sociological analysis of particular situations. The Bank's interventions were inevitably top-down even when they were directed, in intent, to the poorest of the poor.

It is inherently difficult for the Bank to work with small-scale projects. The process of making small loans is costly per dollar loaned. This was a problem even with the top-down poverty programs McNamara pushed. They 'were very staff-intensive; they consumed large amounts of staff time but yielded relatively small loans. . . . It was doubtful at the end of McNamara's tenure whether the Bank could continue to process an ever-increasing number of such relatively small projects.'[16]

Given this problem it is obvious that the Bank was in no position to work with the poor in local communities to help them realize projects they designed and implemented themselves. It had to work through existing top-down power structures or create additional such structures. But in doing so it gave every opportunity for the elite to benefit from their role in development either legally or by illegal manipulation. The 'target' group had no power in the process, and accordingly, it was not the major recipient of the benefits. Furthermore, authoritarian regimes, dedicated to overall economic growth, were ideal collaborators in the process.

It is difficult to be equally charitable in judging McNamara's record on environmental matters. No doubt he was sincere in insisting that they need not interfere with economic growth. Further, under his leadership the Bank did support some environmentally-oriented projects. But at Stockholm he was expressing as fact what could only have been his hopes. His rhetoric gave a profoundly false impression of the extent to which environmental effects were considered at all in the development and approval of Bank projects. At the time he spoke at Stockholm, there was only one environmental advisor in the Bank, and he had no staff support. There was no 'careful set of guidelines.' Even in 1983 there were 'only three people to evaluate some 300 new lending operations totaling over $12 billion a year in addition to monitoring hundreds of ongoing projects totaling tens of billions more.'[17] Clearly McNamara, despite some excellent rhetoric, had no real understanding of the relation of development to environment, or else, at least for practical purposes, he accepted the economistic view that economic growth itself leads eventually to improving the environment.

McNamara's passion was for the poor. He was determined that environmental considerations not deflect the Bank's work for them. And he wanted to assure the Bank's borrowers that he would not allow ecological considerations to interfere with new loans.

In fact the World Bank's projects continued to be environmentally destructive, and the six-fold increase in these projects during the McNamara years only accelerated the devastation. The commitment to increased lending led to great pressure on Bank employees to find nations willing to borrow money and to formulate acceptable projects. Serious attention to environmental consequences would have slowed down this process and, indeed, made this increase impossible. The United States government finally intervened at some points, and reluctantly the Bank increased its attention to the environmental consequences of its projects. It was not until the late 1980s, during the regime of Barber Conable, and as a result of pressure from NGOs, that environmental considerations began to play a significant role in the Bank's efforts.[18]

McNamara was successful in some respects. Some of the Bank's social projects had positive effects. Under his leadership the Bank contributed to bringing inflation under control in such countries as Brazil. In general the Bank prevented net capital flow from shifting away from the South. The vast expansion of loans enabled debtor nations to pay on their earlier loans while still having money for new projects. However, this success in the longer run proved to be part of the growing problem. Increasing the rate of lending to the Third World postponed, but ultimately intensified rather than solved, the problem of debt repayment.

If the huge flow of capital to the developing nations had consistently contributed to real development, this would not be a problem. At some point the prosperity of these countries would be such that they could repay their loans out of profits from the productive facilities for which this money was borrowed. At that point the flow of funds would reverse, the need for new loans would dry up, and the Bank could close down, having accomplished its mission.

No one in the Bank has seriously thought in these terms. By these standards few of its loans had been successful. Only a few countries had reached that stage in development where repayment out of profits was possible.

Furthermore, poverty in the Third World, as calculated by the World Bank, has not been reduced by development, and the gap between rich and poor has grown. The disparity in per capita income between the US and the undeveloped nations is estimated as having been about thirteen to one in 1947. In 1989, after 42 years of development, the disparity had reached around sixty to one.[19] Even more troubling is that disparities within the developing countries have grown, with hundreds of millions of people living in a kind of destitution that was rare in earlier times. Development had removed them from traditional means of livelihood and given them no new basis for self-support.

This problem, still little recognized in Bank literature or practices, is analyzed with particular acuity by Gerard Destanne de Bernis.[20] He points out how what is ordinarily called development renders existing skills irrelevant as well as separating people from their means of production. Regardless of how results appear in overall statistics, these people, previously respected and contributing members of society, are socially marginalized.

If the solution to poverty is the movement of capital into poor countries, then a reverse flow is unacceptable. Yet if loans were to be repaid without this reverse capital flow, the only alternative was continued acceleration of new loans. As long as the new loans continued to have the same effects as the old ones, the spiral of larger lending was the only solution! The larger the lending, the more massive and less considered

the projects for which money was loaned, and the less likely
that the money would reach the poor.

III. THE DEBT CRISIS

The McNamara solution to the problem of debts and their
repayment might have continued to work for some time apart
from other factors in the situation over which the Bank had no
control. The first of these was the 'oil shock' of 1973. The
Organization of Petroleum Exporting Countries (OPEC) was
able to achieve sufficient discipline among its members to raise
oil prices drastically both in that year and again in a second 'oil
shock' in 1979.

This could be viewed as the first successful move by developing countries to take control of the price of their commodities. In this sense it provided them with hope for a shift in the
balance of power in the world. Unfortunately for them, this
did not happen. Eventually OPEC broke down, and no other
organization of commodity producers succeeded. The North
regained full control over commodity prices. In the meantime, the temporary success of OPEC led to a huge transfer of
capital from other Third World countries to the oil producers.
Between 1973 and 1983, the higher price for oil added $250
billion to the cost of their imports.[21]

This by itself would have slowed development in many of
these countries. Paying more for oil left less to pay for other
imports needed for development. Also an increase in the cost
of oil raised the prices of industrial products generally. Hence
it was seriously inflationary. To deal with the higher cost of
goods, Third World countries would have had to tighten their
belts. Growth would have been slowed or stopped.

Eventually the higher price of oil might have had other
effects. It might have shifted energy use to locally available
sources, especially solar ones. By reducing consumption it
would have extended the period during which oil is available
and eased the future transition to a post-petroleum society.
But the whole thrust of development had been to increase
dependence on oil. The Green Revolution had shifted agriculture from solar energy to oil. There was no easy or quick way
to move away from this new, heightened dependence on

imported oil other than economic sacrifice. This could be avoided only by increased borrowing.

It turned out that the transfer of wealth to the oil-producing nations made this increased borrowing easy. Whereas prior to the raising of oil prices, the collective surplus of these countries was around $1 billion a year, in 1974 it was almost $70 billion.[22] The economies of these nations could not absorb this vast capital; so most of the money was deposited in First World banks. In some instances, as in the United States, each dollar deposited in these banks from outside the system allowed the banks to lend ten dollars or more, using the deposits as security. In Europe, where a large surplus of dollars had been accumulated, there was virtually no restriction placed on the amount of "Euro-dollars" that could be loaned. Hence the quantity of money available for loans by commercial banks was enormous.

The economies of the First World countries could not assimilate all of this money, but the profits of the commercial banks depended on making loans. Hence they employed people to go to Third World countries to persuade governments to borrow money for their own use or for government-guaranteed commercial projects. As long as they had government guarantees, the lending banks were little concerned with what was done with the money. Long-term lending to developing countries by commercial banks rose from $3 billion in 1970 to $30 billion in 1981. Short-term lending rose from virtually nothing to $22 billion. Overall, commercial banks, which had been minor players in the field in earlier decades, came to account for around two-thirds of the total capital flow to developing countries.[23]

It is clear, therefore, that despite its great expansion under McNamara, the World Bank was a minor factor in the growth of Third World debt in the seventies. Although one may complain that many of its loans were not effectivly used, in comparison with the commercial loans of the 1973–82 period, they were well-planned and supervised. It was the commercial loans that directly brought about the boom-and-bust from which the Third World has not yet recovered.

We have seen why commercial banks loaned to the Third World. They had money to lend, and the demand was in the developing countries. It was highly profitable to the banks to lend, and as long as the loans were guaranteed by governments, they were not much concerned about how they were used.

The question is, now, why Third World governments were willing to borrow such huge sums. Could they not foresee that repaying them would be a serious problem?

There were several reasons. First, the availability of large amounts of money is inherently attractive. It enables government officials to secure their private future and gain power and prestige. With personal wealth one can escape the consequences that one's nation may bear in the future. In short, some rulers borrowed without concern for national consequences.

As a result, large sums of money were not invested in the borrowing countries at all. Money was deposited instead in First World banks in the private accounts of government officials or others able to profit from the loans. This was not a minor problem. As stated by James S. Henry: 'In some cases, the wealthiest classes of poor countries have actually sent more money out of their countries than foreign borrowing has brought in – and often it's the same money. American banks have promoted, and profited from, both sides of this transaction. Sometimes the money never even leaves the United States. The entire cycle is completed with a few bookkeeping entries in New York.'[24] This is called capital flight, and it has proved an enormous impediment to development. A 1987 study by Morgan Guaranty Trust of New York asserts that if capital flight had not occurred, Argentina's debt would be reduced from $62 billion to $26 billion.

Second, much of the money was borrowed as an alternative to facing very difficult problems in the economy. It enabled countries to continue to pay for needed imports, service their existing debts, maintain and expand their armies, and increase their social services for the poor. These are all normal functions of government, and most governments would choose to borrow rather than discontinue them. The problem, of course, is that these uses of borrowed funds do not build an economic base from which they can be repaid.

Third, even when this was recognized, there did not seem to be much reason for concern. The economies were continuing to grow at a satisfactory rate, and exports even faster. Commodity prices were rising, so that the income for debt repayment could be foreseen. Further, real interest rates were very low, sometimes even negative. In addition, the value of the dollar, in terms of which their debts were stated, was declining relative to other currencies, so that debts could be repaid in cheaper dollars.

Fourth, there were valid investment opportunities in many countries that could generate profit for repayment of loans.

There were, of course, some warnings of problems to come. Even in the favorable climate of the the late seventies, some debts had to be rescheduled. But these averaged only about five a year between 1975 and 1980 with a total value of perhaps $4 billion.[25] This was too small a factor in the total situation to have much effect.

In 1979 two events occurred that changed the climate. First, OPEC again raised oil prices dramatically. This could only fuel the already precarious cycle. Secondly, Paul Volcker drastically raised interest rates in the United States in order to stop inflation and the slide in the value of the dollar. Other First World nations followed suit.

This action affected the finances of Third World debtor nations in several ways. First, it meant that loans would have to be repaid in more expensive dollars rather than cheaper ones. Second the real interest rates on new loans soared from close to nothing to 6 or even 8 percent. Third, since some of the commercial loans bore variable rates, the cost of servicing existing loans rose dramatically. As a result, in 1981, the number of loans that had to be rescheduled increased to thirteen.

In 1982 Mexico was rebuffed by its commercial creditors when it proposed rescheduling its debts. As a result, that summer the government announced that it would have to default on its loans. Since Mexico was one of the largest debtor countries, this shocked the financial world. A default by Mexico would in itself threaten the solvency of some banks. It would probably lead other nations to follow suit. The effects upon the commercial banks that had specialized in Third World loans would be disastrous. The ensuing panic in the financial community in the First World is what is usually called the debt crisis.

This chapter is about the BWI, but this section has described other actors. Still, the Bank and the IMF were not innocent bystanders in the emergence of this crisis. They encouraged borrowing on the part of Third World countries, and in the case of the Bank, pushed its own loans vigorously. Nevertheless, the huge borrowing that brought about the crisis was not from the Bank, and much of it would probably have occurred even if the Bank had disapproved. The Bank cannot be held responsible for either the 1979 increase in OPEC prices or Volcker's decision to raise interest rates and increase the value of the dollar.

Although the debt crisis was not caused by the BWI, their story cannot be told apart from it. It was this crisis that catapulted them into the position of being the most important actors on the world stage at least so far as the Third World is concerned. In evaluating their work today, we must distinguish between the consequences of the debt debacle and the consequences of the remedies they have proposed and imposed. They are too often blamed for both.

NOTES

1. Robert S. McNamara, 'To the Board of Governors, Washington, DC, Sept. 1, 1975,' *The McNamara Years at the Bank: Major Policy Addresses of Robert S. McNamara, 1968–1981*. Baltimore: Johns Hopkins University Press, 1981, p. 309.
2. Robert S. McNamara, 'Address to UNCTAD,' Santiago, Chile, 14 April 1972, p. 4. See J. Kraske, et al., *Bankers with a Mission: The Presidents of the World Bank*. Oxford: Oxford University Press, 1996, p. 197.
3. Ibid., 24 Sept. 1973, p. 261.
4. Ian Bowen and J. Svikhart, eds, *Redistribution with Growth*, a joint study by the World Bank's Development Research Center and the Institute of Development Studies, University of Sussex. London: Oxford Press, 1974.
5. Sheldon Annis, 'The Shifting Grounds of Poverty Lending at the World Bank,' in Richard E. Feinberg, ed., *Between Two Worlds: The World Bank's Next Decade*. New Brunswick, NJ: Transaction Books, 1986, p. 89.
6. Robert L. Ayres, *Banking on the Poor: The World Bank and World Poverty*. Cambridge, MA: The MIT Press, 1983, p. 239.
7. Bruce Rich, *Mortgaging the Earth*. Boston: Beacon, 1994, p. 85. Quoted from Edward S. Mason and Robert E. Asher, *The World Bank Since Bretton Woods*. Washington: Brookings Institution, 1973, p. 306.

8. McNamara, *The McNamara Years*, op. cit., p. 381.
9. Ibid., p. 13.
10. Emmanuel Y. Ablo, et al., *Advancing Social Development*. Washington: The World Bank, 1995, p. xi.
11. McNamara, op. cit., p. 196.
12. Ibid., p. 198.
13. David Beckman, 'Reforming the World Bank: A Personal Testimony,' *The Christian Century*, 16 April 1997, p. 397.
14. Agricultural Missions, *The Christian Rural Mission in the 1980's: A Call to Liberation and Development of Peoples*. New York: Agricultural Missions, n.d., p. 6.
15. David Reed, ed., *Structural Adjustment and the Environment*. Boulder, CO: Westview Press, 1992, p. 14.
16. Ayres, op. cit., p. 249.
17. Rich, op. cit., p. 112.
18. Kraske, op. cit., pp. 267–70.
19. World Bank, *World Development Report 1991*. New York: Oxford University Press, pp. 204–5.
20. G. D. de Bernis, 'Development or Pauperization,' in Paul Mark-Henry, ed., *Poverty, Progress and Development*. London: Kegan Paul International, 1991, pp. 86–137.
21. M. Miller, *Coping Is Not Enough: The International Debt Crisis and the Roles of the World Bank and IMF*. Homewood, IL: Dow Jones–Irwin, 1986, p. 43.
22. Ibid., p. 34.
23. Ibid.
24. 'Where the Money Went,' *The New Republic*, 14 April 1986, p. 20.
25. Miller, op. cit., p. 37.

6 Structural Adjustment

I. THE NEW TASK

The threat of a default on loan payments by Mexico, a major debtor that was also a major factor in world trade, was a very serious matter. Brazil, another major debtor, was considering the same step. Not only would this have serious consequences for some of the world's leading banks, it would also profoundly disrupt trade and investment. The whole system on which global economic development depended was at risk.

Neither the banks nor the debtor nations wanted such disruptions. They wanted to continue much as in the past. The problem was that debt payments had become too large in relation to national resources. Fear that debtor countries would not repay led creditors to resist making further loans. But without large new loans debtors could not continue to pay.

Because of the vast increase in the size of the debt, the problem was much worse than the Pearson report had projected a decade earlier. It was not simply that the reverse flow of funds from South to North would stop Third World growth as new loans failed to keep up with the cost of servicing old ones. It was that new lending stopped abruptly and that without it the old debts could not be paid.

The IMF was called into this difficult situation. Its task was to restore the flow of credit and payments so as to prevent disruption of trade and growth. This was continuous with its initial mission. However, there was in this case no possibility that it lend the debtors sufficient funds to pay their debts. Its approach had to be different.

The most dramatic new feature was the pressure the IMF brought on creditors to extend more credit. Unless they refinanced their loans to Mexico, which involved extending additional credit, they would not be paid. But they were not willing to do this without assurances that Mexico would in fact honor its new obligations. The *quid pro quo* was Mexico's acceptance of stringent IMF conditionalities.

The IMF had developed its conditionalities with temporary problems in the balance of payments in view. Their goal was described as stabilization. However, the conditionalities appropriate to temporary disequilibrium did not suffice to deal with major long-term problems. Hence, the requirements placed on Mexico went much further than earlier conditionalities directed to stabilization. The new requirements dealt with the structure of the whole economy.

In the years since then, the IMF has taken on as its major role in the world guiding debtor nations into the sort of structural adjustments that would enable them to pay their debts and regain economic health. Its resources for doing that, however, are restricted, since it was set up to deal only with limited, shortrun problems.

As noted above, McNamara had earlier concluded that failures of Third World nations to respond well to the stimuli of loans were often based on their social and political structures. To change this situation the Bank had developed a special type of loan for structural adjustment that was quite different from the loans for specific projects that dominated the Bank portfolio. The intention was to enable developing countries to make more efficient use of capital. The IMF turned to the Bank for assistance in funding the adjustments it demanded as conditionalities for its support. In terms of their most important contemporary functions, the two institutions converged on this mission.

There is still some difference in function. The IMF enters the situation initially to help a country deal with its debt problems. Nations that cannot continue to service their debts turn to the IMF as the lender of last resort. The IMF can lend them some funds, but its primary role is to persuade other creditors to extend more credit and to move toward a situation in which other donors and investors will be willing to help. Normally, the Bank now extends credit only with IMF approval. The IMF focuses on the credit-worthiness of the nation, which entails that it is paying its debts, rather than on development.

The World Bank is still directed toward economic development, by which it means, primarily, growth. It functions in a double capacity. It gives long-term loans for structural adjustment. It also continues to make loans, chiefly to structurally-adjusting nations, for development projects. Its purpose in promoting structural adjustment is to provide the context for renewed economic growth. But there is little tension between what is promoted as structural adjustment by the two BWI. Some observers believe they should merge.[1]

Through the intervention of these institutions, the debt crisis, from the perspective of the First World, has been solved. Few banks are now so dependent on Third World loans that failure to pay would be crucial. In part the debts have been transferred to such institutions as the World Bank. In part they have been written off.

To some extent the problem has eased for most Third World debtors as well. Although their total indebtedness is larger than ever, in most instances it is not as large a portion of their national economies. More important, oil prices and interest rates have moved sharply down, and their loans have been renegotiated.

On the other hand, for most of these countries the crisis has been transformed into a chronic burden, especially on the poor. There is no end in sight. The human suffering involved in the 'solution' of the problem continues to be enormous.

II. THE THEORY AND ITS APPLICATION

During their first 25 years, and indeed largely until 1982, the BWI promoted trade and growth with relatively little regard to the political ideologies of the nations they served. Since 1982 and the primacy of structural adjustment, this has been far from true. They now promote a definite economic agenda, that of neo-liberalism, with strong political implications.

This clear commitment to a particular form of economy has several causes. First, since most of the policy-makers are economists, their policies follow from theories they have assimilated in their studies. Second, this economic theory had come to shape the policies of the most powerful nations in the First World, especially the US and Great Britain. The earlier checks on the domination of society by economistic thinking had been overcome, and socialist views had been firmly rejected. Third, the power of OPEC had aroused anxieties among First World leaders about the possibility that the Third World would gain control over other commodities and would undo the gains for the First World that arose from its domination of the global market. Fourth, the logic of debt repayment supported the application of these theories. The standard form of SAPs that have been imposed on most of the Third (and now increasingly on the Second) World follows from this last point. It is important to note, however, that the same policies follow from standard economic thinking in general.

Prior to structural adjustment most Third World nations followed eclectic policies that gave considerable role to nationalism. They generally aimed at healthy national economies. Earlier development theorists had often encouraged them to create import-substitution industries so as to attain more ability to meet their own needs. They developed their own financial institutions as instruments of national policy. Often these industries and financial institutions were government-owned or controlled, but even when they were private, they were protected from international competition.

Sometimes these countries welcomed the investments of TNCs, but usually they maintained some restrictions on them. Concerns about meeting basic needs, promoting health, and raising educational standards influenced their national decisions. At the same time, they pushed exports in order to obtain the hard currency required for purchases from abroad.

These policies were usually in place during the period in which these nations became heavily indebted. They were difficult to sustain without the inflow of funds. Hence the growth they generated could not continue without some assistance from without. When funds ceased to flow in, and debt payments had to be made without the benefit of new loans, drastic action was required.

First, if external debts are to be paid, the country must export more than it imports. Only so will it attain the currency with which to pay. That requires that the nation's capital be devoted to the production of goods wanted by others.

Second, because capital is limited, it must be devoted to producing what that nation produces most efficiently. This is called the principle of comparative advantage. Each nation and each region should specialize in what it can produce most competitively.

Third, negatively, this means that capital should not be devoted to producing what can be more efficiently produced elsewhere. These goods should be acquired through trade.

The nation can acquire more of these goods by exporting what it produces efficiently than by producing both.

Fourth, to assure that capital flows to what is most efficiently produced, the market should be freed from interference by government. That entails selling off government enterprises to the private sector where they must become competitive or else cease to exist. It also includes removing a host of restrictions on the market. For example, government control of the price of food, and subsidies to producers, must end, in order to let the market set prices.

Fifth, the freedom of the market must be extended across the nation's borders. There must be an end of protecting inefficient industries or financial institutions so that, again, resources will be allocated to their most efficient use.

Sixth, the government must raise sufficient funds in taxes to meet its needs and service its debts. This also requires reducing expenditures. One of the most controversial features of structural adjustment is its reduction of government expenditures, many of which are for food, education, and health. But without reduced outlays, either taxes will become so high as to inhibit economic activity or there will be insufficient surplus to service debts.

Seventh, to ensure a surplus of exports over imports without protecting inefficient local production, costs of production must be kept low along with demand for imports. This can be accomplished by lowering wages. Since the need is primarily related to international trade, this goal can be achieved most efficiently by devaluing the currency without raising wages.

These policies favor development as well as debt payment. It is evident that they lower the standard of living for workers while increasing the profit from capital investment. It is capital investment that generates growth. In due course, as such growth occurs, wages can rise again. Loans made in this context will go into capital investment determined by its most efficient use rather than into politically favored projects, servicing debt, or maintaining a standard of living the nation cannot afford.

These policies are also designed to attract foreign investment. With low wages and the removal of governmental restrictions, it is expected that TNCs will establish productive faciltes, chiefly for export, as well as financial services. The former will aid in the achievement of an adequate surplus of exports over imports. The latter will make the handling of finances more efficient. Together they will also bind the nation's economy more tightly into the global one.

Although no one questions that the debt crisis has been the occasion for introducing structural adjustment on a massive scale, its advocates emphasize that the adjustment is needed for development to take place. The debt crisis is not viewed as the reason for the lack of development. That lack results from the distorted structures of these societies. Once the structures are adjusted, it is argued, growth will be the natural result, and the problem of debt payments will decline.

Hence, adjustment is supported on the grounds of its inherent value. Here the power of the economic theory that supports it comes through. This is treated, for the most part, as beyond dispute. Economics is viewed as a science, and mainline neo-liberal economists are understood to have its correct form.

This assumption is made clear in the speech of Lawrence H. Summers to the Bangkok meeting of the World Bank and IMF. He spoke as the Bank's Chief Economist and Vice-President for Development Economics. 'What can the West do to drive this process of reform [in Russia] forward? Number one: it can spread the truth. The laws of economics, it's often forgotten, are like the laws of engineering. There's only one set of laws, and they work everywhere. One of the things I've learned in my short time at the World Bank is that whenever anybody says, "But economics works differently here," they're about to say something dumb.'[2]

Apart from the power of the ideology, one can imagine a quite different response to the debt crisis. Instead of setting aside all efforts that had been made for import substitution, one could have argued for just the reverse. The debt crisis occurred in large part because so many countries were so dependent on imports over whose price they had no control. Over time the cost of manufactured imports has typically risen in comparison with the commodities they exported. The drastic increase of the price of oil threw their economies out of balance. One could then argue that the need was to reduce dependence on international trade and especially on oil and other imports.

This might have been done in part by improving the efficiency of use of oil and oil-based products. Amory Lovins has never tired of pointing out how much can be accomplished along these lines more cheaply than producing or importing new energy. This saving could be achieved both by directly promoting efficient use and also by raising the price of oil. This in turn could be either by a tariff or a quota, with the limits on the amount of oil available forcing the market to set a higher price. It is also possible to develop substitutes for oil, especially forms of solar energy. Countries could also experiment with agricultural practices that are less dependent on oil-based products as Cuba is now being forced to do.

This would not be easy, and it would introduce some disruptions. But it would have been no more disruptive than the changes in the opposite direction imposed by structural adjustment. If a country reduced its oil import requirements by one billion dollars a year, this would be as helpful for balance of payments purposes as increasing net exports by that amount. The environmental effects would be far more beneficial, and the poor would probably be hurt less. At least there would not be the same need to lower wages, and since a shift away from oil generally leads to more labor-intensive production, unemployment might have been reduced.

It appears that the problem with this approach was not that it was less feasible but that it would not lead in the direction of the global market so prized by economistic thinkers. Import substitution leads to more self-reliant national markets. Also, the reduced consumption of oil is likely to show up negatively in the GDP. Nevertheless, prior to the debt crisis and structural adjustment, the record of growth by countries that had included an import-substitution strategy in their planning was not inferior to those that had emphasized exports.

It should be noted that this is not an argument against structural adjustment as such. Much that was called for by SAPs was needed. Government-owned industries are often inefficient. They should at least be forced to compete on an equal basis with privately-owned companies. Many countries favored some sectors of the population, usually those closest to political power, in unjust and economically destructive ways. SAPs usually pushed in the direction of greater fairness. The point here is only that structural adjustment could have aimed at developing more independent and self-reliant economies rather than at greater dependence on trade and external investment.

III. THE INCREASE OF POVERTY

Unless the volume of investments and new loans to a structur- ally-adjusting nation is very large, the new policies necessarily resulted in a net transfer of capital from the 'developing' country to its creditors. This is inherently entailed in the pay- ment of debts. During the 1982–6 period there was a net outflow of resources from Latin America amounting to $132 billion.[3] From the Bank's perspective, this was a temporary evil to be mitigated by loans and to be replaced as soon as pos- sible by new growth. The IMF also wanted its policies to pro- duce growth.

Similarly, these policies are designed to reduce the standard of living of the people as a whole, that is, their level of con- sumption. Since we are speaking of countries in which many were already desperately poor, this cannot be taken casually. During the 1982–6 period, per capita income in Latin Amer- ica declined 7.5 percent.[4] Given the nature of the policies that produced this decline, it was the workers who paid the price, not the investors.

The situation in Africa was worse. In 33 African countries betwen 1980 and 1989 'average GDP percapita...fell 1.1 percent a year, while per-capita food production also experi- enced steady decline. The real value of the minimum wage dropped by over twenty-five percent, government expendi- tures on education fell from $11 billion to $7 billion and prim- ary school enrolments dropped from eighty percent in 1980 to sixty-nine percent in 1990. The number of poor people in these countries rose from 184 million in 1985 to 216 million in 1990, an increase of seventeen percent.'[5]

The Institute for African Alternatives held a conference in London in 1987 on 'The Impact of the IMF and World Bank on the People of Africa.' The focus was on SAPs. Participants concluded that 'in virtually all cases, the impact of these pro- grammes in African countries has been basically negative. They have resulted in massive unemployment, falling real incomes, pernicious inflation, increased imports with persistent trade deficits, net outflow of capital, mounting external debts, denial of basic needs, severe hardships and de-industrialization.'[6]

The conference pointed out that most of the proposals that have been made to alleviate the suffering share the basic assumptions underlying SAPs. For this reason they are only ameliorative. What is needed is to clarify the fundamental problems and respond to them. To this end it recommended 'that alternative programmes and solutions should be premised on the rejection of the conventional theory of economic growth and foreign capital.'[7] The need is to elaborate 'an alternative grassroots-oriented strategy of national and collective self-reliance that is not autarky to restore basic autonomy and security to African economies.'[8]

The initial purpose of SAPs had not been to deal directly with present human needs. This concern of McNamara moved to the periphery under his successors. The purpose had been to maintain the global system of trade and finance as the orderly basis for economic growth everywhere. The BWI knew that they were requiring sacrifices, but they believed these to be necessary. A popular phrase has been 'No pain, no gain.' Still economistic thinkers expected the period of suffering to be brief. They anticipated rapid economic gains from the structural changes that were implemented.

Nevertheless, many in the Bank were disturbed by the depth and protracted nature of the setbacks that the reforms brought about. A 1990 World Bank discussion paper put it this way: 'In the early years of adjustment lending there was optimism that adjustment programs would be temporary, and that with the resumption of growth poverty would continue to diminish and the adverse social effects of adjustment would be remedied. But, because the economic problems were more severe than expected, implementation of adjustment programs has been less successful than anticipated and many countries have experienced prolonged periods of economic stagnation and deteriorating social conditions for some groups. This situation has led the international development community to renew its attention to poverty reduction.'[9]

Noteworthy is that, for the authors, the problems do not cast any doubt on the basic wisdom of the SAPs. This is underscored in the 'Abstract' where we read, as very often in World Bank literature: 'One clear lesson from experience has been that an orderly adjustment process designed to establish a new equilibrium growth path is indispensable for improving the longer-term position of the poor.'[10] This means, presumably, that breaking down barriers to trade and investment is necessary to overcoming poverty. This 'clear lesson' seems to be learned more from the ideology than from historical evidence.

In 1991 the Bank adopted a poverty-reduction strategy. This called, of course, for continuing economic growth. But the Bank now recognized that projects designed to promote growth should also directly promote employment. They should be labor intensive. Second, the Bank would support investments in human resources through health and education. Third it would provide safety nets to prevent extreme suffering from economic deprivation.

This double message of the importance of export-led growth and of fine-tuning the policies that generate it is conspicuous in the 1996 report by the Bank on its work to reduce poverty.[11] In the list of lessons learned by the Bank, the first is 'how important growth is to reducing poverty.'[12] But the report also details programs in childhood education and lending to the poor that are not the standard ways of promoting growth. Furthermore, it assures us, the 'Bank's support for adjustment operations has become more specifically poverty-focused over time. In addition to including measures to protect or increase social sector expenditures, the Bank's adjustment operations are also increasingly including provisions to put safety nets in place to support those most affected during the process of economic reform and transition. Operations are also including more active measures to reduce economic distortions that disproportionately hurt the poor. The Bank is working to improve, for example, its knowledge of how adjustment affects women and to change its operations to address the issue.'[13]

Despite the fine-tuning of SAPs to reduce poverty, the results are thus far mixed. A 1995 report of the Operations Evaluation Department (OED),[14] while generally affirming of the effects of structural adjustment on poverty reduction also notes that the Bank frequently fails to assess adequately the actual causes of poverty and that such good assessments as are made fail to shape Bank lending. The report states that 'country assistance strategies [have] focused on broad macroeconomic stabilization and structural reform issues, with few references to the status or causes of poverty.'[15]

There is, thus, a double response to the disruptive consequences of structural adjustment. The Bank is committed to its basic principles, but it also seeks to moderate their negative effects by modifying the policies and by supplementary activities. Critics believe the negative consequences should lead to fundamentally questioning some of the assumptions underlying SAPs and to new policies based on different principles.

The continuing difference between the perspective of the Bank and its Earthist critics appears in the 1994 World Bank Group celebration of its first fifty years: *Learning from the Past: Embracing the Future*,[16] on the one side, and Oxfam's *A Case for Reform: Fifty Years of the IMF and World Bank*,[17] on the other. The former is a highly up-beat document pointing to the great global progress made in Third World countries during this half-century: longer life expectancy, increased schooling, and doubling of average income since 1960. With regard to SAPs the book acknowledges that adjustment is more complex than originally expected, that it is more dependent on historical variables, and that it takes longer than anticipated. But the picture projected is one of achieved success in some places and anticipated success elsewhere. There is no hint of uncertainty as to whether these programs are desirable.

A striking contrast in perception relates to Latin America. In the World Bank document we read: 'Many countries (especially in Latin America) are prospering in the new global environment. Their trade with the rest of the world is increasing, they have become more sophisticated in economic management, and many are progressively less dependent on official sources of finance.'[18] Oxfam, on the other hand, reminds us that during the decade of adjustment (1980–90) World Bank figures themselves show a rise in poverty from 27 to 33 percent. It charges that 'the Bretton Woods Institutions have remained oblivious to the connections between these trends and adjustment policies.'[19] Instead of viewing the growth of trade and improved fiscal management hailed by the Bank as reassuring, Oxfam says that its 'experience suggests that SAPs offer a future of "growth through exclusion", leaving the poor increasingly marooned among islands of prosperity.'[20]

Whereas the Bank's report views Sub-Saharan Africa as lagging behind because of difficulties in full application of SAPs, Oxfam points to ways in which following SAPs has directly damaged them. It comments that 'the imposition of "export-led growth" strategy for resolving the debt has carried the seeds of its own destruction, especially in the world's poorest countires. By expanding production of commodities such as coffee, cocoa, tea for world markets which were already oversupplied, structural adjustment programmes contributed to the most protracted and deep depression in the world markets since the 1930s.'[21]

IV. A TEST CASE – GHANA

Judgment of the merits of SAPs with their heavy emphasis on the global market is central to the concerns of this book. It is almost impossible to resolve by empirical evidence. Economistic thinkers ask whether increase in per capita GDP has followed from structural adjustment. Bank thinkers also ask whether there has been a reduction of the number of people receiving less that a dollar a day. The answer is that by these standards there have been improvements in some structurally adjusted countries, but not in all. In any case it is difficult to determine the extent to which changes of this sort, good or bad, are the result of the SAPs and to what extent they are determined by other causes.

Since the implementation of structural adjustment is never perfect, and since there are always unrelated problems in each country that contribute to economic failures, believers in standard IMF/World Bank SAPs can always claim credit for successes and blame failures on lack of full implementation or extraneous factors. According to Ishrat Husain, the Bank's study of the situation in Africa[22] 'demonstrates (1) that there is considerable variation in economic results of adjustment programs among African countries and (2) that this variation is explicable in terms of the quality and sustained application of adjustment policies.'[23]

Even if structural adjustment could be proved to be consistently successful by strict economistic standards and by those of the World Bank, Earthists who advocate a quite different type of development would not be satisfied. For Earthists it is important that people participate in the economic decisions that shape their lives and that communities be relatively self-reliant rather than primarily dependent on remote centers of economic power. Instead of relying on external investments for development, they favor local self-determination. They are especially concerned for self-sufficiency in food and for sustainable use of natural resources. In their eyes, some features of the standard SAPs work directly to undercut these goals. From this perspective, the recent eforts of the World Bank to mitigate the adverse human and environmental costs of structural adjustment are admirable, but they do not touch the core issue of whether nations should be forced to open their borders to the free movement of capital and goods.

The actual effects of SAPs can be better evaluated in case studies than in overall statistics. Ghana is rgarded by the World Bank as one of its relative success stories. It is one of two African countries in which 'there has been a steady implementation of reforms.'[24] The Bank explains the fact that, nevertheless, economic progress from 1983–94 was limited by noting that 'the more deep-seated reforms that will encourage private sector investment – both domestic and foreign – have not yet sunk in.... The prospects for sustained long-term development will not improve unless the forces of private initiative and enterprise are unleashed and the state plays a more supportive and facilitating role.'[25]

In 1992 the *World Bank Economic Review* published a study based on a survey of 82 manufacturing firms, entitled 'How Small Enterprises in Ghana Have Responded to Adjustment'[26] This shows that the removal of tariffs and subsidies and lowering the value of the Ghanaian currency have negatively affected the large industries that government had heretofore favored. The 'restraints on demand' inherent in standard SAPs, combined with pushing more people into private work by reducing employment in government and industry, led to greater difficulties on the part of microenterprises. The one hopeful sign was successful adjustment on the part of firms employing from 4 to 29 full-time workers. Some of these showed successful entrepreneurial leadership and had the possibility of growth if credit were available for expansion.

A still less encouraging view of Ghana is provided by Fantu Cheru[27] 'While statistics may suggest significant economic improvement in that country, a deeper and broader assessment of the effects of structural adjustment yields a very different view.'[28] The chief success of the restructuring was the recovery of cocoa production for export, but this was offset by decline in the price of cocoa which accompanied higher prices for imports.

A serious issue with regard to reducing poverty is the distributional effect of support for cocoa production. Ninety-four percent of the gross income from cocoa was received by 32 percent of the cocoa farmers or about 6 percent of the farming population.[29] Because incentives are not directed to the production of food for the local population, an activity in which women predominate, Ghana's self-sufficiency in this important area has declined. Meanwhile Ghana's 'debt rose from $1.1 billion in 1980 to $3.4 billion in 1988.'[30]

'To make up for declining foreign exchange earnings from cocoa, the timber industry is being revived with support from the World Bank.... This has accelerated the steady destruction of Ghana's forests.'[31] There is danger of virtually total deforestation with disastrous consequences for food production.

Summarizing his study of Sub-Saharan Africa, Cheru writes: 'conventional adjustment policies, while improving output for export crops, have often aggravated poverty, income inequalities and environmental degradation. Government support to agriculture has mainly favored large farmers who produce for export to the disadvantage of small farmers who produce food for local consumption. Beyond reinforcing the conditions that perpetuate rural poverty and inequality, these reform measures are contributing to deforestation and soil erosion by directing productive resources, money and valuable personnel toward the export-producing sector for short-term gains. Meanwhile, small farmer go on exploiting degraded land for lack of technical support in agroforestry, soil conservation and food production.'[32]

The deeply different perceptions of the effects of structural adjustment led the World Wildlife Fund to commission studies of structurally adjusting countries. Its intention was to achieve as much objectivity as possible in evaluating the positive and negative contributions of these programs to sustainable development with a special emphasis on the environment. They deal with the sort of macroeconomic issues more characteristic of Bank studies than of NGOs. Two volumes have appeared embodying its findings: *Structural Adjustment and the Environment*[33] and *Structural Adjustment, the Environment, and Sustainable Development*.[34] The first reports on studies of three countries: Côte d'Ivoire, Mexico, and Thailand. The second reports on an additional nine.

The editor, David Reed, defines sustainable development as improving the quality of human life while living within the carrying capacity of supporting ecosystems.[35] He examines sustainble development in terms of its economic, its social, and its environmental components. Although this broad approach is more characteristic of the Earthist perspective than that of the World Bank, it builds on positions acepted in principle by the Bank. He writes:

> The economic component of sustainability requires societies to pursue economic growth paths that generate an increase in true income, not short-term policies that lead to long-term impoverishment. Further, it means that societies generate an optimal flow of income while maintaining their basic stock of capital. Economic sustainability also implies internalizing all costs, including the societal and environmental costs associated with the production and disposition of goods, thereby implementing the full-cost principle.
>
> The social dimension of sustainable development embodies the fulfillment of basic human needs and equity of opportunity. For a development path to be sustainable over a long period, wealth, resources, and opportunity need to be shared in such a manner that all people have access to minimum standards of security, human rights, and social benefits, such as food, health, education, shelter, and opportunities for self-development. Social equity means ensuring that all people have access to education and the opportunity to make productive, justly remunerated contributions to society.
>
> The environmental dimension of sustainable development is predicated on maintaining the long-term integrity

and therefore the productivity of the planet's life-support systems and environmental infrastructure. Environmental sustainability requires that environmental goods and services are used in such a way as not to diminish the complex inter-related functions of nature or the overall contribution of environmental goods and services to human well-being.[36]

Reed discovered that better pricing structures resulting from structural adjustment have had some beneficial results. But overall his conclusions support NGO objections more than World Bank defenses. SAPs benefit the rich at the expense of the poor, who are forced into environmentally destructive practices, some of them irreversible. They speed up the exhaustion both of soil and of mineral resources. They are socially destructive.

Macroeconomic studies of the results of SAPs are import-ant, but personal judgments are often formed more by lived experience. India will serve as a final example of opposing perceptions. Recent developments there are widely celebrated in the press as India enters the global market and its GDP rises rapidly. Things look different through the eyes of a Presbyte-rian agricultural missionary, Brooks Anderson.

Rural Indian society is being severely destabilized as land reform legislation is repealed; as satellite dishes bring American TV shows to even the most remote villages; as mul-tinational corporations set up enormous corporate farms to produce food for export and to meet the growing demand for highly processed and highly profitable junk food; and as the environment collapses under the pressure of the rapidly growing population. Some of this change is being demanded by the World Bank as part of the structural adjustment program which is just one of the strings at-tached to their loans. Some of the change has been designed by those Indians who have much to gain if their society is restructured according to the logic of trickle-down economics.

In cities it is easy to see many of the results of economic liberalization, which is making small numbers of Indians richer while keeping a growing percentage of the popula-tion in subhuman living conditions. Across the road from my house, the squatter slums grow each day like cancer around the industrial estate where children are employed for as little as twenty-two cents per day. Meanwhile the industries' managers come and go in their air-conditioned Japanese and Korean automobiles.[37]

Impassioned anecdotal accounts such as this are difficult to relate to the overall statistics about poverty, the distribution of income, and the environment which shape the judgments of World Bank staffers. Such personal reports often increase at just those times when economistic thinkers are claiming the greatest success. However one may judge their value for informing policy decisions, they are unquestionably important in explaining the rising tide of hostility to the BWI that will be the topic of the following chapter.

NOTES

1. See George B. Burnham, 'Understanding the World Bank: A Dispassionate Analysis,' in Doug Bandow and Ian Vasquez, eds, *Perpetuating Poverty: The World Bank, the IMF, and the Developing World*. Washington: Cato Institute, 1994, p. 84. George P. Schultz, 'Economics in Action: Ideas, Institutions, Policies,' *American Economic Review*, May 1995, pp. 5–6. Raymond F. Mikesell, *Revisiting Bretton Woods: Proposals for Reforming the International Monetary Institutions*. Annandale-on-Hudson NY: Jerome Levy Economics Institute of Bard College, 1996, p. 33.
2. S. George and F. Sabelli, *Faith and Credit: The World Bank's Secular Empire*. Boulder: Westview, 1994, p. 106.
3. Carlos Geraldo Langoni, *The Development Crisis: Blueprint for Change*. San Francisco: International Center for Economic Growth, 1987, p. 52.
4. Ibid., p. 57.
5. George and Sabelli, op. cit., p. 141.
6. Bade Onimonde, *The IMF, the World Bank and the African Debt: the Social and Political Impact*. London: ZED Books, 1989, p. 191.
7. Ibid., p. 193.
8. Ibid.
9. Helena Ribe, et al., *How Adjustment Programs Can Help the Poor: The World Bank's Experience*. Washington: The World Bank, 1990, p. 1.
10. Ibid.
11. Lynne Sherburne-Benz, *Poverty Reduction and the World Bank: Programs and Challenges in the 1990s*. Washington: The World Bank, 1996.
12. Ibid, p. xii.
13. Ibid.

14. World Bank Operations Evaluation Department, 'Structural Adjustment and the Poor,' Oct. 1995.
15. 'Leaked Report Scores World Bank Poverty Assessments,' *BankCheck Quarterly*, Dec. 1996/Jan. 1997, p. 6.
16. *Learning from the Past: Embracing the Future.* Washington: World Bank Group, 1994.
17. *A Case for Reform: Fifty Years of the IMF and the World Bank.* Oxford: Oxfam Publications, 1995.
18. *Learning from the Past*, p. 11.
19. *A Case for Reform*, p. 10.
20. Ibid.
21. Ibid., p. 7.
22. World Bank, *Adjustment in Africa: Reforms, Results and the Road Ahead.* Oxford: Oxford University Press, 1994.
23. Ishrat Husain, *Why Do Some Economies Adjust More Successfully Than Others? Lessons from Seven African Countries.* Policy Research Working Paper, 1994, p. 2.
24. Ibid., p. 3.
25. Ibid., p. 35.
26. William F. Steel and Leila M. Webster, 'How Small Enterprises in Ghana Have Responded to Adjustment,' *The World Bank Economic Review*, Vol. 6, No. 3, 1992, pp. 423–38.
27. Fantu Cheru, 'Structural Adjustment, Primary Resource Trade and Sustainable Development in Sub-Saharan Africa,' *World Development*, Vol. 20, No. 4, April 1992, pp. 497–512.
28. Ibid., p. 506. Cheru refers to Donald Rothchild, ed., *The Political Economy of Ghana.* Boulder, CO: Lynne Reiner Publishers, 1991.
29. Cheru, op. cit., p. 507.
30. Ibid.
31. Ibid.
32. Ibid.
33. David Reed, ed., *Structural Adjustment and the Environment.* Boulder, CO: Westview Press, 1992.
34. David Reed, ed., *Structural Adjustment, the Environment and Sustainable Development.* London: Earthscan and Washington: Island Press, 1996.
35. David Reed, *Executive Summary: Structural Adjustment, the Environment and Sustainable Development.* Washington: World Wildlife Fund, p. 5.
36. Ibid., pp. 5–6.
37. Brooks Anderson, 'Global Economics at Work in the Indian Countryside,' *Fellowship*, July–Aug. 1997, p. 20.

7 A Coherent Opposition

I. EARLY RESISTANCE

During the first quarter-century of their operation critics might disagree with particular policies of the Bretton Woods institutions, but there was no significant popular opposition. Global economic development was seen as highly desirable, and the World Bank, in particular, was seen as playing a positive role, if not a very conspicuous one. Idealists concerned themselves with prodding national governments in the First World to lend and give more generously to Third World Nations, assuming that most of the money was well-spent. They also organized their private relief and development organizations.

Even in those years there was moral outrage over some of the actions taken in the name of development. Most of these actions were taken by authoritarian governments usually controlled by the military. They typically suppressed labor movements and kept wages very low so as to gain competitive advantages for fledgling industries. They sometimes built massive infrastructure projects ignoring the suffering of those who were displaced. These policies evoked resistance from those who were exploited and protests from their supporters both at home and abroad. In some cases opposition eventually led to the overthrow of military regimes and the restoration of more responsive governments.

McNamara's predecessor, George Woods, headed the World Bank from 1963 to 1968. He believed that 'the main objective of the Bank was to help countries to achieve development through improved economic management.'[1] The loans, credits, economic studies, and technical studies through which the Bank sought this end appeared complementary to other development efforts.

However, even technical advice could be controversial, especially when it was linked with offers of aid. India was a major focus of aid programs for the international community, and it was a country of particular interest to Woods. The donors had become dissatisfied with Indian progress under its successive five year plans, and World Bank representatives were among those to voice criticism.

One problem was that India had exhausted its foreign exchange and was running deficits in its trade. The Bank recommended devaluing the rupee and reducing bureaucratic control of the economy. The implication was that continued and increasing aid was contingent on moving in this direction. In a mild form, this anticipated the later SAPs. The recommendation and implicit threat aroused strong opposition in India. Indira Gandhi eventually agreed to devaluation, but its effects were far less beneficial than had been hoped. The central planning of the economy continued, partly because 'donors were unwilling to help the Bank to come up with the required package of inducements.'[2] Suspicion of the World Bank in the developing world gained a focus.[3]

Woods also initiated Bank involvement in the Green Revolution and succeeded in getting the Indian government to support it. 'As a result, within a few years India moved from being a food importer, threatened by famine whenever the monsoon failed, to being self-sufficient in food.'[4] There can be little doubt that this greatly benefited the economy of India overall. On the other hand, it had socially and environmentally negative effects and left India more dependent on imported oil.

These problems were minor, however, in comparison with the McNamara years. 'Under Woods, the focus was on what the member country could do for itself with the help of the Bank; under McNamara and his successors the volume of loans became the objective.'[5] This favored large-scale projects less carefully planned and with little input from the people affected.

Throughout this period there were many nongovernmental development agencies. Their work was typically small-scale and community based. They usually emphasized the participation of local people in their own development. Although in some instances the massive intrastructure projects favored during the McNamara years could be viewed as complementary to this bottom-up development, increasingly they were seen as in conflict. Those who had worked at village development were appalled when the villages in which they had worked were scheduled for flooding and resettlement for the sake of a dam that would benefit only distant people.

Earlier, when development projects detrimental to local interests were introduced by private capital, people could appeal to their government. If their government rejected their appeals, or in instances where the government itself was the developer, opposition would be directed at it. But McNamara led the Bank to take the lead in projects of this type. Hence, the Bank became a major object of protest for grassroots movements throughout the developing world and for the agencies in the West devoted to community development.

This does not mean that these NGOs opposed all the Bank's efforts. Far from it. Many of the McNamara initiatives in behalf of the poor were appreciated. Their protests were focused on specific projects, usually very large ones, which they were convinced did more harm than good.

II. THE ENVIRONMENTAL MOVEMENT

Meanwhile a new dimension was added by the burst of ecological awareness into the popular consciousness. Earth Day 1970 gave expression to the new concern. Numerous organizations were founded or took on new life, and they have gained considerable influence. For most of them, the fundamental aim of economism at endless economic growth did not ring true. Preserving or restoring the health of the Earth seemed of primary importance. The World Bank as one of the most visible institutions devoted to economic growth was an obvious target of criticism.

Other parts of the environmental movement had more limited aims. They sought to preserve particular ecosystems, or protect tropical forests, or defend the habitat of endangered species, or reverse the pollution of air and water, or reduce the erosion of topsoil. These wanted the Bank to cease supporting activities that were destructive in these respects. For example, they raised massive objections the Bank's support of Brazilian policies that were rapidly decimating the Amazon forests. They wanted the Bank instead to give positive support to environmental goals. To these requests the Bank has been increasingly responsive.

Those committed to the poor and oppressed were suspicious of the new movement. At the time of the first Earth Day, there were many who feared that love of the Earth led to less concern for poor and oppressed human beings struggling for liberation. They noted that extreme language about danger to the planet as a whole made concern about distribution of goods seem of secondary importance.

These suspicions were not altogether misplaced. After so long a period of anthropocentrism, some environmentalists, or Earthists, opposed the well-being of the Earth to the quest for human well-being in misanthropic ways. Also, some saw humankind in general as the enemy, the cancer that is killing the Earth. Believing the planet to be overpopulated, some were callous toward the victims of plagues and famines. Although these voices were a minority among the Earthists, they were loud enough to cause alarm.

The World Council of Churches (WCC), for example, distanced itself from the first UN meeting dealing with the environment (Stockholm, 1972). Many of its members understood environmentalism to be a First World concern that distracted attention from the struggle for justice. However, by 1975, at its own meeting in Nairobi, the WCC had come to recognize that ecological sustainability is important for all, and it added 'sustainable' to 'just' and 'participatory' as descriptive of the society to which it is committed. Since that time it has given effective leadership among Christians all over the world in showing the interconnectedness of justice, participation, and a sustainable relationship to the natural world.

Whereas the alleviation of poverty could be viewed as the central purpose of the Bank, environmental concerns were peripheral. Chapter 5 described McNamara's continued devotion to overcoming poverty and his apparent assumption that environmental concerns could be dealt with quite simply and peripherally. Clausen was less open to environmental concerns, and such attention as the Bank directed to the environment in the early eighties was widely viewed as a concession to external pressure rather than as growing out of its own thinking and purposes.

Clausen's successor, Barber Conable, was personally much more committed to deal seriously with the environment than any of his predecessors. It was in his administration that environmental programs were massively expanded. Nevertheless, even his administration gave the impression of yielding to pressure rather than being proactive.

The typical thinking of many of the Bank's most idealistic leaders through the eighties, and even into the nineties, can be illustrated by quoting, once again, from Lawrence Summers, this time from his review of *Beyond the Limits*. He wrote: 'The environment is a critical global problem. Environmental problems are serious everywhere, but it is only in poor countries that they kill and disable millions of people each year, which occurs on top of the other crushing effects of poverty. Any strategy for addressing environmental concerns that slows the growth of poor countries either by regulating them directly or by limiting their markets is grossly immoral.'[6]

This statement reflects the widespread conviction among economists that growth, measured in terms of GDP, is essential to the reduction of poverty. To use envirnomental concerns as a reason for restricting growth is, therefore, 'grossly immoral.'

That this has in fact been the dominant position of the Bank is shown in the 1992 World Development Report (WDR). This provides a fine summary of environmental problems. But a careful study by David Reed leads him to the conclusion that the Report's call for managed growth as the solution at no point considers 'that more and better managed economic growth will fail to solve the environmental crisis. Despite a predicted 3.5–fold increase in global productive outputs and a population increase of 3.7 billion people by 2030, the WDR denies, without sound analysis, that there are growth frontiers. Any resource or absorptive constraints imposed by the physical environment can, according to the WDR, be addressed through new technological innovations, substitutions of new products, and (undefined) structural changes.'[7] In short, the Bank has understood these matters largely according to the same orthodox neo-liberal economic theory in terms of which Summers wrote.

Still, there is no question that the Bank's interest in the environment has increased. Just as, beginning with McNamara, it ceased to suppose that overall economic growth is the only needed response to poverty or to population growth; so it also recognized that overall economic growth is not the only response needed to environmental deterioration.

The Bank worked hard to gain a leadership role in the Global Environment Facility (GEF) for which it shares responsibility with the UN Development Programme and the UN Environmental Programme. Its chairing of the Facility exposes it to critical evaluation by the environmental community. Having sought and accepted this role it is unlikely that the Bank will return to the cavalier disregard of the environment, based on economistic assumptions, that earlier characterized many of its policies. The real test is how it directs the new Environmental Facility.

In the view of David Reed, the fundamental question is whether the investments of the GEF 'are addressing energy issues of marginal importance...while neglecting to tackle the underlying economic and institutional problems that are largely responsible for creating the global environmental crisis in the first place.'[8] Thus far, he thinks, the answer is Yes. But this need not be the last word.

III. NONGOVERNMENTAL ORGANIZATIONS

Differences in basic perspective and perception do not prevent authentic communication between the Bank and NGOs. Despite the fact that the participation of affected persons and effects on the environment are not directly relevant from a purely economistic point of view, the Bank has undertaken to deal seriously with them. Hence the NGOs have a strong interest in working with the Bank to help it become more participatory and more effective in reducing damage to the environment. To varying degrees over the years the Bank has welcomed NGO advice and assistance. Already in 1982 the Bank established the NGO-World Bank Committee as a forum for discussing how 'the Bank could increase the involvement of NGOs in bank-financed projects. In the mid-1980s, the Committee shifted its focus toward more policy-related areas.'[9]

Participation by NGOs in Bank projects has increased steadily over the years. 'Operational collaboration between the World Bank and NGOs has greatly intensified over the

last decade. While only six percent of all Bank-financed projects in the period 1973–1988 included provisions for some
form of involvement by NGOs, NGOs were to be involved
in about 30 percent of all Bank-financed projects in FY93,
and between 40 and 50 percent of projects approved in FY94
and 95. . . . The Bank is striving to increase both the quantity
and the quality of NGO involvement in Bank-financed
projects.'[10]

The Bank acknowledges that in at least half of these cases,
NGOs had no share in the planning of the projects. 'The Bank
is aware that if NGOs are expected to participate in a meaningful way, it is important that they have a say in the design
of the project, including defining the terms of their own
involvement.'[11]

NGOs vary immensely in their interests, their size, and their
modus operandi. Sometimes they work in opposition to one
another. Tensions remain between those concerned with justice and those that focus on the health of the environment, but
conflict among NGOs has been progressively replaced by
cooperation.

Despite the serious efforts of the Bank to improve relations
with NGOs, many of them continued to be suspicious of its
programs and the ways they were decided on. As the years
passed more and more NGOs became clear that development
policies largely guided by the Bank were of particular concern. They discovered that the projects that were most disturbing to those who came from the side of community
development and liberation struggles were also most disturbing to those who were chiefly concerned for the fate of the
natural world. Finding themselves allies, they began to act in
concert.

Opposition to the Bank's projects has often centered on
large dams. These have played a major role in Bank lending.
According to *Damming the Rivers: The World Bank's Lending for
Large Dams*, a report by International Rivers Network, in
'more that 100 cases . . . loans made for large dams were, at
the time of approval, the single largest loan for any purpose
made to the borrowing country.'[12] Until recently environmental considerations played a minor role in the process of
making these loans. And although the Bank has long had
official commitments to the just resettlement of all those

forcibly removed from their homes, the actual record is often tragic.[13]

The most extended protest was directed to the the Sardar Sarovar Dam Project in India, initially granted $450 million in 1985. The project would require relocating 90,000 people, most of them tribals, as well as flooding agricultural land and forests and disrupting the entire river eco-system. Opponents focused attention on the consequences of building the Narmada Dam. They also pointed out that the Bank was not following its own policies in these matters.

These policies called for study of alternative ways of achieving essential goals. They also included stringent requirements of justice in resettling displaced persons. And, in calculating costs and benefits, environmental losses were supposed to be taken seriously. None of this had been done. The NGOs representing the victims in India joined forces with international groups concerned with justice and with the environment in a persistent campaign to force the Bank to abide by its own rules.

There is no court of appeal beyond the Bank to compel it to comply. Nevertheless, the NGOs were able to bring considerable pressure to bear directly and through some of the Bank's national directors. Finally, Barber Conable appointed an Independent Review team, headed by Bradford Morse. The team recommended suspension of Bank participation, especially because the adequate resettlement of those to be displaced was not possible under existing circumstances. Forty-one percent of the shareholder executive directors, including the US, supported the report.

However, in September 1991, well before the report was completed, Conable had been succeeded by Lewis Preston, who advocated ignoring the report and continuing the incremental policies that had thus far failed. He won a majority vote and gave India an additional six months to improve the situation. The day before its report was due, India requested that the Bank cancel the remaining $170 million of its original commitment.

The struggle continues in India itself, because the withdrawal of the Bank leaves open the likelihood that the project will be carried forward in humanly and environmentally destructive ways by the Indian government. The Save the

Narmada movement has blocked construction temporarily through the courts, with the final outcome still uncertain. Regardless of the actual results on the ground in India, the outcome at the Bank encouraged the NGOs, and it showed them how similar the interests of many of them are on major issues of development. What is bad for local communities is usually bad for their environments, and what is bad for the environment is bad for the people who inhabit it. In addition, it led the Bank to establish an internal Inspection Panel to which those adversely affected by the Bank's projects could appeal.

The alliance formed around opposition to large top-down development projects has been cemented by the experience with SAPs. Chapter 6 emphasized their negative effects on the poor and the environment, at least as seen by Earthists. This shared perception has led to concerted action.

IV. THE TWO PARADIGMS

Many of the same NGOs that have shared in opposing mega-projects and SAPs worked together to plan and implement the NGO 'Global Forum' that parallelled the 1992 UN Earth Summit at Rio de Janeiro. While the US delegation prevented significant action from taking place at the Earth Summit, maintaining the global economistic system intact, the Global Forum hammered out a series of 'treaties.'

BankCheck Quarterly quotes Walden Bello as saying that 'these treaties address issues completely ignored at the Earth Summit, such as the roles that debt, multilateral lending institutions, and transnational corporations play in perpetuating development that is bad for the environment and the people it is intended to help.'[14] That thousands of people coming from many organizations in many countries could come so quickly to consensus indicates that there is convergence around a development paradigm quite different from the one that dominated the official Earth Summit.

The dominant paradigm of development is 'economistic' in that it focuses on economic growth, measured by GNP or GDP. It assumes that economic growth as thus measured is good for people. In its purest form it argues that other valid social goals such as poverty-reduction, full employment, wages and workplace standards, quality education and health care, population stabilization, environmental protection, and democratic government are by-products of this economic growth. Even when some of these claims are muted, the primary emphasis on economic growth is retained, and separate attention to these other concerns can be regarded as a distraction.

In this economistic perspective, growth is obtained by freeing markets from government restrictions both internally to nations and between nations. This leads to more efficient use of capital. Developing countries in addition need new infusions of capital. This may come from gifts or loans, but increasingly it comes from investments by transnational corporations. Since far more capital is available from private than public sources, the role of public institutions is primarily to insure that nations make themselves attractive to private investors. For example, the BWI may pressure developing countries to abandon restriction on foreign ownership, and they may insure investors against losses due to changes of governmental policies.

The NGOs have observed the consequences of the application of this paradigm in developing nations, and they are distressed by what is happening both to the people and to the environment. They have become convinced that large-scale, top-down development concentrates wealth in fewer hands, transfers power to TNCs, destroys traditional communities rather than developing them, disempowers the poor, and degrades the environment. They propose a different model.

In this model, policies aim directly at human well-being conceived much more broadly. The health of human and natural communities is more important to such well-being than the amount of average consumption of goods and services by individuals. The people to be helped are especially the poor, and they are helped best by empowering them to help themselves. Although governments are often corrupt, there is a better chance of popular concerns being expressed through them than through TNCs; so power should not be transferred to the latter.

This model can recognize the advantages of market mechanisms overagainst excessive bureaucratic management of the economy, but its emphasis is on local markets instead of the global market. Strengthening local markets can help people to become more self-reliant and more nearly self-sufficient, reducing their dependence for necessities on decisions made at distant places. Traditional concerns to preserve the local environment are to be encouraged and emphasized rather than set aside for the sake of growth. Even in judging narrowly economic gains, environmental losses are to be seriously considered.

In short, this model is bottom-up, seeking to improve the human condition in general by improving that of the Earth including the human communities that can thrive only as the natural systems also thrive. Economic 'growth' that genuinely contributes to the well-being of human communities in a sustainable way is welcomed. But this growth will be very different from that aimed at by the economistic paradigm. This emerging NGO model is Earthist.

This Earthist model has support far beyond the NGOs. A recent statement by James Gustav Speth, the Administrator of the UN Development program, expresses his full agreement. He comments that when 'we speak of a "new paradigm" or a "new model of development", it can sound top-down, imposed. This new paradigm is anything but top-down, indeed, it is just the reverse. It is the world screaming back at us. It is screaming back in hunger, in pain, across the wastelands and dead waters. Only the purposefully deaf have not heard it.'[15] His formulation of the Earthist paradigm, which he calls 'sustainable human development' is classic.

> Sustainable human development is, first of all people-centered. It puts poor people first. It meets their basic needs, including the need to attain self-reliance, and it enlarges their opportunities, including the opportunities to live a long and healthy life, to be educated, and to have the employment needed for a decent standard of living.
>
> Sustainable human development is also environmentally sound. It stresses the need to regenerate the natural resource base, to increase the long-term productivity of the resource sectors, and to protect the environment both locally and globally. And sustainable human development is participatory, it can only be achieved where people have an

opportunity to participate in the events and processes that shape their lives.[16]

V. WHERE THE BANK STANDS

The World Bank was established by economistic thinkers for economistic purposes. At the same time, these purposes were formulated in unusually idealistic ways. The goal of poverty-reduction has been taken seriously by many of its leaders, and when it became clear that economistic policies by themselves did not accomplish this goal, the Bank gave it separate attention. Similarly, under McNamara the Bank realized the population issues must be addressed directly. Later, environmental problems also claimed and received such attention. Programs for improved education and health care certainly do not await the attainment of a certain level of per capita income. Many of the projects undertaken out of these concerns have strong support from those who adopt the Earthist paradigm.

On the other hand, attention to these concerns has not led to rethinking the basic economistic paradigm. Indeed, commitment to supporting the emergence of the global market at which that paradigm aims became the dominant factor in Bank policy in the eighties. Hence, the paradigm determinative of the Bank's policies can be described as maintaining the basic economistic circle with the addition of epicycles.

This language comes from the theory about the movement of the heavenly bodies in the ancient world. Deeply entrenched in the classical mind were the convictions that the heavenly bodies had a perfection lacking in earthly ones and that the perfect motion was circular. Initially this gave an adequate approximation to the observations of the actual movements, but as these observations became more accurate, discrepancies were found. To avoid abandoning the perfection of the circular movement, small circles were superimposed upon the large one. These are the epicycles. For centuries astronomers employed the paradigm of cycle and epicycle to account for the data without abandoning the basic theory.

The use of epicycles is itself paradigmatic. When a theory is maintained by superficial adjustments to counterevidence, it functions as a cycle on which epicycles are affixed. From the perspective of Earthists, this characterizes the thinking of the Bank. Together with most economists, most governments (especially that of the US), most international agencies, and most TNCs, the Bank believes that the primary requirement for development is a smoothly functioning global market freed from unnecessary interference by governments.

More clearly than most of its partners, the Bank recognizes that single-minded pursuit of this goal fails to solve urgent problems. But this recognition does not lead to basic questions about the appropriateness of the underlying aim. Instead, this aim continues to guide most policies, while obvious needs not met by these policies are given separate attention. They are epicycles that do not affect the basic model. This will be spelled out in more detail in the next chapter.

VI. FIFTY YEARS IS ENOUGH

At Rio many of the NGOs, especially those in the US, attained a coherent opposition to the dominant approach to development. They became clear that they were operating out of a very different paradigm from the economistic one that dominated the official conference. The Earthist paradigm they adopted was directly in opposition to the neo-liberal economistic paradigm held by the government of the US and imposed on the basic decisions of the 'Earth Summit.'

The Bank's experience in dealing with the poor and with the environment had already led it to modify this paradigm significantly. Nevertheless, it was the Bank that was the chief public agency for global development, and in directing this development it had been dominated through the years by economistic thinking. From the NGO perspective, the practical effects of this thinking had grown worse in the eighties.

First, the BWI had been assigned responsibility to prevent the debt crisis from hurting the First World banks without receiving significant financial help from First World governments. The resulting solutions they imposed on debtor countries placed the chief burden on the poor and on the environment. These solutions systematically forced the integration of national economies into the global one. Second, the Bank continued to support large-scale, top-down projects, especially dams, that were, from the perspective of the NGOs, harmful both to the poor and to the environment. Third, whereas in the first decades after World War II, First World governments had committed themselves to aid Third World countries by grants and loans, the US led in reducing this commitment and turning development over to investment by TNCs. The Bank aided and abetted this process. Developing countries were more and more controlled by these corporations.

In addition to the judgment that much of the Bank's work did more harm than good was the frustration often felt by the NGOs in dealing with it. Although they were given opportunities to make proposals, the outcome often ignored their contributions, and they were unable to learn what had happened and why. The apparent openness to their input often seemed a smokescreen designed to deflect their criticism. Even national governments sometimes found the decision-making processes of the Bank to be hidden.

For reasons such as these, despite acknowledging the real concern of the Bank to reduce poverty and its growing interest in social and environmental matters, and despite approving many of the Bank's projects, an important group of US NGOs decided to engage in a campaign of confrontation and opposition. They chose to focus on 1994, the fiftieth anniversary of Bretton Woods, naming their campaign 'Fifty Years is Enough.'

Despite the implications of the name, its purpose was not in fact to bring an end to the BWI, leaving lending and investment entirely to the TNCs. But the campaign did aim to break deepseated habits and approaches that have characterized the IMF and the Bank through most of their history.

The platform of the US Campaign[17] followed from the implications of the Earthist paradigm. It aimed both to reduce the size of the institutions and to redirect their operations. Since size is in itself one of their problems, often motivating lending beyond any real need and certainly beyond the abiity of the lender to monitor effectively, there is a positive connection between these two elements.

The platform calls for: 1. 'Openness and full public accountability of the Bretton Woods institutions and the systematic
integration of affected women and men in the formulation,
implementation, monitoring and evaluation of World Bank
and IMF projects and policies.' This would transform the
ethos and style of the institutions which have been accustomed
to secrecy and to little accountability outside themselves. Projects would have to be justified in open discussion with those
who will be affected by them.

In principle Bank leaders have been increasingly supportive of public accountability and transparency. Michael Bruno,
who succeeded Summers as chief economist, wrote: 'The
World Bank's policy is clear; we recognize and endorse the
fundamental importance of accountability and transparency
in the development process. . . . Dissemination of information
to local groups affected by projects supported by the Bank,
including non-governmental organizations, will facilitate the
participation of these groups in Bank-financed projects.'[18]

The problem was less one of official policy than of effective
implementation. This implementation is improving. Furthermore, the Bank has had a growing commitment to the participation of those affected by projects, recognizing that project
success often depends on this participation. The critics were
attacking observed past practice rather than official Bank policy and improving practice.

2. A major reorientation of the World Bank- and IMF-
financed economic-policy reforms to promote more equitable
development based upon the perspectives, analysis and development priorities of women and men affected by those policies.' This would transform structural adjustment. Lending
would now 'serve to: a) strengthen a wide variety of productive activities of the rural and urban poor; b) increase rather
than diminish local self-reliance, broad-based demand, and
workers' rights and wages; c) promote broad-based sustainable food production by increasing access to land, credit and
other productive resources for small farmers and microenterprises; d) directly address women's lack of access to resources
and decision-making structures and promote equity in the
development process for all disadvantaged groups; e) ensure
environmental sustainability by decreasing the rate of natural-
resource extraction, increasing regulatory oversight and pro-

moting end-use efficiency in the energy and water sectors; and f) allow for increased investment in much needed physical and social infrastructure, especially health care, education and economic opportunities for women and girls.'

The World Bank could honestly state that it is already committed to many of the specifics listed here. But it now treats these as epicycles on its SAPs. The Campaign calls for a reversal. These epicycles *are* the needed structural adjustment. This would free the Bank to work for reduced natural-resource extraction which is quite different from the effects of its current policies.

The sharpest challenge to Bank intentions in this plank of the platform and the next is the call for promoting local economic self-reliance. This idea is notably absent from Bank rhetoric, because it directly challenges economistic thinking.

3. An end to all environmentally destructive lending and support for more self-reliant, resource-conserving development that preserves biodiversity.' Among the implications drawn from this is a moratorium on large dams as well as an emphasis on alternative projects that achieve the needed results and on greater efficiency in the use of currently available energy and water.

The Bank already intended to minimize the environmental destructiveness of its projects, conserve resources, and preserve biodiversity. Its difference from its critics is that it aimed to do this in the context of increasing economic activity everywhere in an ever more unified global market. Supporters of the Fifty Years is Enough campaign believed there was a deep contradiction involved. The Bank remained committed to large-scale infrastructure projects such as dams, believing that the problems with these projects were being considered much more adequately than in the past.

4. The scaling back of the financing, operations, role, and hence power of the World Bank and the IMF and the rechanneling of financial resources thereby made available into a variety of development assistance alternatives.' The Campaign calls for scaling back both institutions, denying future capital requests, and separating IDA and GEF from the Bank.

The Bank is open to reducing its bureaucracy and working toward greater efficiency and effectiveness, but not to scaling back its activities or losing control of IDA or GEF.

5. A reduction in multilateral debt to free up additional capital for sustainable development.' The Campaign urges the IMF and the World Bank to use their reserves to write off the debt owed them by the poorest countries. It also proposes writing off debts on financially failed projects, of which, by the Bank's own calculations, there are many. This would discourage the Bank from continuing to make questionable loans, whose failures add to the burdens of the poor who must repay the Bank that pushed the failed projects without consultation with them.

At the time of the campaign it was often stated that no debt-forgiveness by the BWI was possible, but more recently this has changed. Of course, the Bank can reasonably assert that it has learned from its mistakes in past investments and works constantly to improve the quality of its portfolio.

VII. THE RESULTS OF CONFRONTATION

In addition to mobilizing, educating, and directing unfavorable publicity at the BWI all around the world, the Campaign had some success in bringing political and economic pressure to bear on them during 1994. The House of Representatives eliminated US funding for the IMF's Enhanced Structural Adjustment Facility, complaining about IMF secrecy and protesting the results of structural adjustment. Some funding of Bank programs was made conditional on reforms. SAPs came under strong attack especially in preparatory discussions leading up to the World Summit for Social Development. The UN Secretary General, Boutros-Boutros Ghali, stated that SAPs 'must be designed to be socially and environmentally sound ... [and] be tailored to local conditions' and should be 'complemented by equally powerful initiatives to ensure that adjustment is not carried out at the expense of the poor.'[19] Barney Frank convened a meeting of 23 parliamentarians from 18 World Bank member countries with responsibilities for oversight. All complained of the lack of information provided by the Bank. Although handicapped by this lack of information, most believed that SAPs have done more harm than good.

Nevertheless, overall, the Campaign was not seriously threatening. The BWI continue to be financed. At the insistence of the US, the shift of economic power from the UN to the BWI, consistent with economistic thinking, continued. Discussion of structural adjustment, so prominent in preliminary meetings, was excluded from the World Summit for Social Development. It occurred only in the accompanying NGO conference whose Copenhagen Alternative Declaration argued that the 'dominant neo-liberal system as a universal model for development has failed.'[20] Boutros-Boutros Ghali, for his failure to support US policy, has been denied a second term. And the G-8 remains strongly behind the BWI and structural adjustment as instruments of fostering world trade and the global market.

Meanwhile there is an understandable backlash against the NGOs in the Bank. 'The Bank's senior management overturned months of work on a new strategy paper for cooperation with NGOs in August 1994, opting for a less sweeping, "business as usual" approach.'[21] A two-year-old fund for innovative social and humanitarian initiatives was not renewed. Senior management also considered 'the option of a decisive retreat from rhetorical commitments on poverty and participation, which some feel have given external critics too much leverage over the institution.'[22]

On the other hand, the Bank did take actions responsive to the NGO complaints. 'As a major step to increase access to the Bank's information, in January of 1994 the Bank opened a Public Information Center that responds to requests from interested parties for a variety of documents, ranging from staff appraisal reports and environmental assessments to descriptions of individual projects under preparation.'[23]

The Bank's willingness to improve relations with NGOs despite their harsh criticisms is shown by its also establishing in 1994 a Task Force on Operational Collaboration. This includes senior Bank managers and representatives of NGOs which have had experience working with the Bank. The Bank also supports conferences organized by NGOs relevant to the Bank's broader objectives.

Futhermore, during the period of the Fifty Years is Enough campaign, the Bank's commitment to many of the goals of that campaign grew. It focused extensively on health and education and the reduction of poverty. It increased its efforts to involve affected people in its projects and to consider their social consequences. And it committed itself strongly to the protection of the environment and of biodiversity. By the conclusion of the campaign the gap between NGO demands and Bank intentions, if not always Bank practice, had narrowed.

NOTES

1. Andrew W. Kamarck, 'Foreword,' in Robert W. Oliver, *George Woods and the World Bank*. Boulder: Lynne Rienner Publishers, 1995, p. xi.
2. Ibid., p. xii.
3. The story is told in detail in Oliver, op. cit., Chapter 5.
4. Kamarck, op. cit., p. xii.
5. Ibid., pp. xi–xii.
6. S. George and F. Sabelli, *Faith and Credit*. Boulder: Westview, 1994, p. 110.
7. David Reed, *The Global Environment Facility*. Washington, DC: World Wide Fund for Nature, 1993, pp. 29–30.
8. Ibid., p. 28.
9. Claudia Fumo, *The World Bank's Partnership with Nongovernmental Organizations*. Washington: World Bank, 1996, p. 5.
10. Ibid., p. 6.
11. Ibid.
12. J. Majot, 'New Report Slams Bank Dam Record,' *BankCheck Quarterly*, Dec. 1994, p. 12.
13. See e.g. Michael Cernea, *African Involuntary Population Resettlement in a Global Context*. Washington: World Bank, 1997.
14. 'No More Than a Dream in Rio,' *BankCheck Quarterly*, July 1992, p. 1.
15. James Gustav Speth, 'Seeking a New Consensus on Development,' NGO/DPI Annual Conference, General Assembly Hall, United Nations, 8 Sept. 1993.
16. Ibid.
17. This can be found among other places as an insert in *BankCheck Quarterly*, June 1994.
18. Michael Bruno, 'Statement' to Multinational Group of Parliamentarians in Oversight of the IMF and World Bank, US House of Representatives Subcommittee on International Development, Finance, Trade and Monetary Policy of the Committee on Banking, Finance and Urban Affairs, 21 Nov. 1994, p. 5.
19. Martin Khor, 'Summit Slaps SAPs,' *BankCheck Quarterly*, Sept. 1944, p. 5.
20. 'UN Social Summit Sapped,' *BankCheck Quarterly*, May 1995, p. 15.

21. Paul J. Nelson, *The World Bank and Non-Governmental Organizations.* New York: St. Martin's Press, 1995, p. 184.
22. Ibid., p. 185.
23. Bruno, op. cit., p. 5.

8 The Development Paradigm of the World Bank

I. THE BANK'S NEW PARADIGM – SUMMERS

Chapter 7 spelled out the Earthist paradigm in contrast to the economistic one and stated that the Bank's paradigm is somewhere between the two. It argued, however, that it is closer to the economistic one despite its concern for the Earth including the people who dwell in it, especially the poor. It stated that from the Earthist point of view, it can be seen as the economistic paradigm with Earthist epicycles.

The image of cycle and epicycles can be viewed as a hopeful one. It is unstable, since there is no coherent overall theory. But its instability can lead to such a theory, one that gives up the commitment that leads to the incoherence. The question that underlies this examination of the Bank is whether a new paradigm can emerge within the Bank that is closer to the Earthist one. To answer that question this chapter will examine the thinking of leaders in the Bank from 1990 to 1995, showing the epicyclic character of their paradigm. The following chapter will examine hopeful developments during that period and the changing rhetoric and practice introduced by the present president, James Wolfensohn.

The Bank has not spelled out its basic paradigm of development in an official way. There are, however, useful unofficial statements. One is developed quite fully by Summers in 'A New Development Paradigm.' Even though he gave this speech after he left his position as Chief Economist of the Bank, his account seems congruent with the actual policies of the Bank.

Summers' paradigm has three elements. The first is the familiar economistic one. 'Markets work. Capital responds to incentives.'[1] Throughout the speech from which this is quoted, it is clear that a major part of the new paradigm will be to continue supporting the flow of investment into developing countries from developed ones. Every indication here is that with respect to this capital flow, more, in almost any form, is seen as better.

The second element is putting people first. 'Investments in people, the one resource countries can't import, are the most fundamental investment for long run economic growth.'[2] This is clearly a distinct point from the first, since most capital flows are not directed to the health and education of the people. It is not a sharp break from previous Bank policy, however, since health and education have been supported strongly since McNamara. This is the point where the programs of the Bank often have the greatest NGO support.

Nevertheless, it is significant that investments in people are for the sake of economic growth. No doubt, Summers assumes as beyond question that economic growth is for the sake of people. But the needs of people other than increased production and consumption are little discussed.

Summers does want to improve the Bank's practice with regard to putting people first. In addition to investment in human resources, putting people first is 'a matter of putting people at the center of the development process. Affected communities must be recognized as constructive partners in the development process. That can only happen if new ways are found to mainstream public participation in project selection, design and implementation. There should also be a renewed Bank–borrower partnership to ensure that the benefits of "grassroots" experiences find their way into lending operations. This isn't just a matter of morality or values. It is proven experience that incorporation of local knowledge vastly improves the quality of projects.'[3]

This is surely a promising emphasis, and one that follows from the Bank's own studies. One such study dealt with water systems in the dry Himalayan foothills of Nepal. Most of these have been built by aid agencies, including the Bank, which, seeing the need, sent in engineers to do the work. A Bank study showed that 'at least 80 percent of the water systems built in Nepal break down after just three years.'[4] The same study showed that 97 percent of the water systems built by World Neighbors are still working after 15 years.

'The key to success has been community involvement and ownership from the beginning. World Neighbors and its local partners work with the villages from the outset to design the system, mapping out where they think water taps should be placed and setting up local user and maintenance committees to ensure the long-term viability of the systems. Villages donate their own labor and some of the materials so they will feel a sense of ownership.'[5]

If the Bank would really allow local communities to propose projects and would be guided by those communities in their implementation, the change would move it a long way from the economistic top-down to the Earthist bottom-up paradigm. It would, however, raise questions about Summers' commitment to promoting the maximum flow of private capital into the Third World, a consequence to which Summers seems oblivious. In short, his recognition of the need to pay attention to local wisdom is a long step from economistic to Earthist ideas of development, but it falls short. Summers' new paradigm would turn to people and local wisdom as a means to attain growth defined economistically. It does not yet grasp that people must participate in their own development. It does not recognize that true people-centered development will often subordinate economistic growth to other values. Since what the poor want is likely to be incompatible with the TNC investments celebrated by the Bank as the major means of development, it is very difficult for it to listen to what they say. The Bank knows from the economic theory to which it subscribes that it knows better than the poor what will benefit them.

The third element of the new paradigm involves weaving environmental considerations 'into the fabric of economic policy.'[6] This is exactly what environmentalists hope for. But it is not clear that Summers understands fully what would be involved. If environmental considerations were part of the fabric of economic policy, the first of the three elements of Summers' paradigm would require modification. Markets are valued because of their contribution to increasing economic activity. Environmental considerations often call for reducing economic activity.

To integrate environmnetal considerations into the fabric of economic policy would be to reorient that policy toward meeting more human needs with less market activity. That would not exclude the market from an important role. But it would favor a reduced role and smaller markets. There is no indication that Summers is ready for that.

Since it seems unlikely that Summers intends either the call for participation or the integration of environmental considerations to alter the basic commitment to economic growth achieved through the globalization of the market, these added elements should be understood as having a subordinate role. As Muhammad Yunus, founder of the Grameen Bank in Bangladesh, noted: 'the theoretical framework within which the World Bank operates does not assign any urgency or primacy to poverty reduction. As a consequence, its pronouncements about poverty reduction get translated only through humanitarian add-ons, such as safety-net programs.'[7]

Thus, despite all of the shared concerns, the Bank and Earthists see the world in different ways. Summers' new paradigm is the old neo-liberal economistic one with epicycles. The addition of the epicycles is valuable and important. But Earthists call for subordinating the aim at growth to broader considerations of human betterment rather than viewing human betterment as a means to growth or growth as the basic means to such betterment.

II. PERCEPTIONS OF MEGAPROJECTS

One function of a paradigm is to provide a way of seeing. The world appears different to those who see it through economistic lenses and those who see it in an Earthist way. The Bank's perceptions differ from both, but have been closer to the economistic.

The Bank's perception can be illustrated from Summers' speech. At one level he has heard the concerns of the Bank's critics. He assures his audience that 'new policies for bank lending regarding forestry, energy, agricultural, and water resources now govern bank activity. Sound resettlement guidelines protect the rights of local populations. The first highest environmental priority is ensuring absolute and full compliance with all environmental policies. That will mean no more Narmadas.'[8]

Those who have been pained by the Bank's past failure in these areas are glad to hear of this resolve. But when

Summers says there will be no more Narmadas, he does not necessarily mean that the bank will cease financing similar projects. This might result if water systems were planned in full consultation with the people immediately affected or if environmental considerations were woven into the planning. In most instances, local people and environmentalists would highlight low cost, small-scale, alternatives, but Summers shows no interest in these. Summers means only that, when the Bank builds dams, it will be more careful to follow its own guidelines and more careful to insist on compliance with all agreements, especially with regard to resettlement of displaced people, by the recipient government.

That commitment to mega-projects and especially huge dams continues is clear from more recent Bank actions. 'In April 1994 the Bank loaned $460 million to China to build the Xiaolngdi Dam, a $3.5 billion project that will displace 200,000 people and function for only 20 years. The Bank approved this loan the same year it was revealed that Chinese authorities disappeared at least 179 activists who were opposing another project, the massive Three Gorges Dam, and that the government was recommending a special secret police force to provide a "swifter and heavier punishment policy against any conspiracies aimed at disturbing the construction."'[9]

Perhaps the Bank has followed all of its procedures, studied the environmental impact of this dam carefully, and done adequate cost accounting. At least IDA has provided a $110 million credit supporting resettlement of 181,000 people, and there are indications that the Chinese government will insure that they will be humanely resettled. Still, it is hard to imagine that the Bank has consulted these persons who will be displaced by the dam. Even if all Bank policies have been followed, those who view reality through Earthist eyes see this as bad development. Given the Bank's record, it is disheartening to learn that yet 'another 600,000 people will be uprooted by projects awaiting approval through 1997.'[10]

The human and environmental destructiveness of these megaprojects has been demonstrated again and again, and the persistence of the Bank in supporting them has caused great frustration over decades. Conable acknowledged in 1987 that 'the World Bank has been part of the problem in the past.'[11] As a result of recognizing responsibility, the Bank formulated new policies to deal with specific problems, and it declared its resolve in future not to ignore its own rules.

The basic economistic understanding of development leads the Bank to support projects of this type proposed by its member governments. Given the assumptions that China needs a great deal of economic growth and that the real choices are hydropower and coal, a case can be made for damming China's great rivers. The World Bank's involvement in such projects typically leads to higher standards both environmentally and in terms of resettlement than those followed in projects in which the Bank plays no role. The epicycles are beneficial.

Summers seems to ask that critics trust a Bank, which has not always been trustworthy in these respects in the past, to police its own actions. Yet at the time that he was assuring his hearers that there would be no more Narmadas, the Bank was engaged in a somewhat similar process. It was supporting a hydropower project in Nepal called Arun III.

Opponents of Arun III appealed to the Bank's Inspection Panel. The Panel found merit in their case and called for a full-scale investigation, including full consideration of alternatives. In the same year that Summers assured his hearers that there would be no more Narmadas, the Bank declined to consider such alternatives.[12] The social and environmental problems in this instance were far less serious than those associated with the Narmada dam, and Summers had no responsibility for the Bank's decision not to follow all the recommendations of its Inspection Panel. Nevertheless, this incident raised questions about how fully the Bank could be trusted to follow the procedures and observe the safeguards it had itself developed to insure that there would be no more Narmadas.

The point is not that leaders in the World Bank who declined to follow all of the Inspection Panel's recommendations were immoral or stupid. They may well have been behaving rightly in terms of their own vision and values. Their concern is to put large sums of money to work for the prosperity of poor countries. Dams that provide electricity and water for irrigation appear to them excellent projects. A single large centralized project of this sort can be supervised and managed more easily than many small projects. Also, unlike some other projects, they often generate revenues from the sale of electricity and water that enable borrowers to repay in a timely fashion. Excessive concern about the social and ecological disruptions entailed seems sentimental and distracting from the central task. In general the Bank's commitment to borrowers seems morally weightier than some procedural irregularity. As long as social and environmental concerns are only epicycles that do not change the basic model, it seems better to move ahead and make the necessary adjustments as time passes.

Although such thinking on the part of those who operate with the Bank development paradigm can be understood and respected, it cannot be accepted by those who approach matters in an Earthist way. It is for this reason that the NGOs have to be vigilant and, at times, confrontational. Until the participation of those most affected and environmental concerns become basic parts of the Bank paradigm, instead of epicycles to it, the NGOs must remain alert.

III. PERCEPTIONS OF PROGRESS

Differences in perception show up still more vividly in the appraisal of what has happened to the world, especially to the poor, in the past fifty years. Summers rightly asserts that the Bank 'has been at the center of the post-war world's development effort'[13]; so an appraisal of the effects of this effort is also an evaluation of the World Bank and its policies. He views the results as a resounding success.

He writes: 'The human condition has changed more in the last half-century than in any previous century in human history. A child born in the developing world today is half as likely to die before the age of 5, twice as likely to learn to read, and can expect more than twice the material standard of living of a child born just a generation ago.'[14]

We are again dealing with the clash of two worldviews, two religions, two spiritualities, or two preanalytic visions. The Bank is an institution of economism, established to further its ideals. Its leaders have represented, and today represent, the most humane advocates of these ideals, deeply committed to improving the lot of the poor and, increasingly, to conserving the environment as well. They believe that the policies the growth-oriented policies they pursue have had, and continue to have, these results and that, indeed, they constitute the only way to accomplish these goals. Despite the increasing role of the epicycles in the Bank's thought and practice, their basic conviction is based on economistic thinking.

Earthist critics see matters quite differently. They join in celebrating the global gains in life expectancy and literacy, but they do not see these as resulting from free international trade, TNC investments, and the increase of global production. The gains have resulted from programs directly targeted on making health care and education available to the global poor, programs for which the Bank can take considerable credit. They see the improvement as more closely connected to equity than to total product.

The critics point out that early in the 'development' period Sri Lanka achieved high levels of life expectancy and literacy without economic growth while remaining aloof from the global market. Cuba measures very well by these standards despite its poverty and its imposed isolation from the global economy. The Indian state of Kerala, with the same per capita product as India in general, has been far more successful by these measures.[15] On the other hand, it is possible for per capita income to rise quite high with little benefit to the masses in terms of life expectancy and literacy.

Summers' assertion that a child born into the developing world today can expect more than twice the material standard of living of a child born just a generation ago is his translation of statistics showing that per capita GDP in developing countries has doubled during that period. This reflects the typical economistic mindset which Summers has in some respects transcended. Although he knows that per capita GDP does not really measure the material standard of living, he falls back into the habit of using these statistics as if they did. The need for statistics that take account of the misleading character of GDP is accented by this statement on his part.

For example, Summers has acknowledged that the loss of natural capital should be considered in national income statistics, and figures adjusted for this loss would be quite different. In principle, he would probably recognize, along with many economists, that much of the growth in GDP goes into 'defensive' expenditures, that is, costs connected with the growth itself. This should be subtracted before calculation of economic well-being. He might acknowledge that if one factored in non-market production, such as household work and subsistence farming (work done chiefly by women), the apparent growth would turn out to be much less. He is explicit that increased military expenditures should not count as adding to material well-being. Clearly taking such matters into account would change the statistical outcome. One could no longer argue from the fact that GDP per capita has doubled in developing countries to the conclusion that people in those countries are twice as well off.

Summers may assume that the difference made by more accurate figures would be trivial, but in fact it is not. For example, the development by Redefining Progress of the Genuine Progress Indicator has shown that in the US the latest doubling of per capita GDP has not been accompanied by any actual improvement in sustainable economic well-being for the people as a whole.[16] This is partly for the sorts of reasons noted, but also because increased income and wealth have been concentrated in the top twenty percent of the population.

This problem of distribution of income is even more acute in some developing countries, and it is acknowledged elsewhere by Summers himself. He knows that more than a billion people live in extreme poverty. Children born in this context will not have twice the material standard of living of those born a generation ago. Many of are then worse off by standard economic accounting, that is, even without taking into account the many further deductions that should be made. When full accounting is done, many others whose cash income is slightly higher than before will also be seen to have lost more than they have gained. On the other hand, children born to the wealthy in these countries may have five to ten times the material standard of living enjoyed by the rich a generation ago.

Critics further note that the nature of poverty has changed. Fifty years ago most people in the developing world lived in rural villages. By the standards of the developed world they were very poor. The process of development has uprooted many of them from the countryside. Hundreds of millions now live in slums surrounding enormous cities. Their condition is vividly described by Robert D. Kaplan in 'The Coming Anarchy: How scarcity, crime, overpopulation, tribalism, and disease are rapidly destroying the social fabric of our planet.'[17] They may, on average, have a slightly higher income than standard measures attributed to them when they lived in rural villages, and they may have more access to education and medical care. But those who view the situation through Earthist eyes conclude that the overall quality of their lives has deteriorated.

In typically economistic fashion, Summers draws other significant implications from his use of per capita GDP to determine how well off people are. He concludes that it is unwise and even unethical to make sacrifices in one generation for the sake of future ones as Earthists sometimes propose. 'Our grandchildren,' Summers writes in a letter to *The Economist*, 'will in all likelihood be much better off than we are. While nobody can accurately predict long-term growth rates, remember that standards of living are three times higher than 60 years ago in the United States, seven times higher in Germany and almost ten times higher in Japan. Should my American grandparents have reduced their standard of living, when life was considerably more nasty, brutish and short than now, to leave raw materials in the ground for my benefit?'[18] Summers' appeal is to concern ourselves for today's poor, not our rich descendants. But one issue, from an Earthist perspective, is whether, even if his doubtful expectation of endlessly increasing GDP is correct, consuming more food, more automobiles, and more houses than the plenty most of us already enjoy will compensate our descendants for the social decay, the degraded environment, the hotter climate, the absence of wilderness, and the reduced biodiversity that we will bequeath them.

Even the increased life expectancy that has been achieved since World War II is not an unmitigated blessing. Given the threat of overpopulation, it is a good only when it is accompanied by lowered birthrates. There has been some progress in this field, and the Bank has contributed to it, but it has been far from sufficient to stop the population explosion.

IV. PERCEPTIONS OF STRUCTURAL ADJUSTMENT

Views of structural adjustment are likely to follow closely on those of progress generally. SAPs were initially and primarily for the sake of maintaining and expanding the global financial and trade system. Secondarily they were for the sake of improving the efficiency of national economies and their attractiveness to foreign investments. The kind of growth hailed by Summers when he states that people in the Third World are twice as well off as they were a generation ago is facilitated by these changes.

Structural adjustment, thus, is integral to the pursuit of growth through international trade and investment. It is not surprising, therefore, that Summers does not hold it, in principle, responsible for increasing poverty. Nevertheless, he recognizes that SAPs could be improved. 'Clearly, we've learned a great deal about the adjustment process over the past 15 years. One of the things we've learned is that the quality of deficit reduction is just as important as the quantity of deficit reduction. Deficit reduction has to focus on those areas which are a real waste, like military spending. And responsible sustainable adjustment programs must protect necessary social programs.'[19] In this way structural adjustment can, and should, be 'fine-tuned.'

Along with purely economistic thinkers, the Bank believes that SAPs that lead to integrating national economies into the global one are necessary. It sees no alternative to temporary 'discipline' for the sake of restoring long-term economic growth based on participation in the global market. The critics, from past experience and day-to-day observation, doubt that in many countries present suffering will lead to future prosperity for the poor, or that present degradation of the environment will lead to its future health. They call for policies aimed directly at benefiting the poor and the environment now. They would adjust debt repayment, foreign investment, and international trade to the needs of the poor for access to the means of production, self-reliance, health care, and education.

From the Bank's perspective, this is sentimental. Since the only long-term hope for the poor lies in strengthening the global economy, autonomous local economies have to be sacrificed, wages must be lowered, unnecessary workers must be fired, and consumption must be restricted through depreciating the currency, removing government subsidies and adding sales taxes. For economistic thinkers there is no other way, and they believe that this one has been proven to work. The suffering thus inflicted on the poor can be alleviated by specific programs targeted to their benefit. From the perspective of the critics, these programs have been shown over and over again to concentrate wealth in fewer hands, make the poor totally dependent on a system they cannot influence, and destroy the environment from which they have subsisted.

V. THE PRESTON YEARS

Michael Bruno succeeded Summers as chief economist at the Bank. In general his policies and vision were similar, but on major points his commitment to the primacy of growth as the means of solving human problems was less qualified than Summers'. Like Summers and the Bank generally, he strongly supported lending for 'good quality education, health, nutrition, and family planning services.'[20] Thus investment in people is an essential complement of the broad-based, labor-intensive economic growth at which the Bank aims. The primary goal is the alleviation of poverty.

On the other hand, Bruno was critical of efforts to improve Third World labor and environmental standards by imposing requirements upon them. Instead, the focus should be on economic growth. 'Experience shows that development is in general the most powerful mechanism for raising standards: As incomes rise households demand better standards and both households and societies can afford to pay for them. ... Thus, reforms which promote economic growth in the developing world will also help to improve working conditions and provide a better environment. Similarly, the evidence supports the argument that shifts towards greater openness to trade and capital flows for a given country tend to promote better rather than worse environmental performance.'[21] Although Bruno concedes that with regard to labor standards and the environment 'there is also room for targeted complementary interventions – as for poverty reduction,'[22] it is clear that these epicycles play a smaller role in his thinking than in that of Summers.

Lewis Preston was president of the Bank from 1991 to 1995. Under his leadership the Bank published its vision of its mission on the fiftieth anniversary of its founding. Preston himself describes the five main challenges facing the Bank.[23]

Pursuing economic reforms that promote broad-based growth and reduce poverty.

Investing in people through expanded, more effective programs for education, health, nutrition, and family planning – so that the poor can take advatage of the opportunities that growth creates.

Protecting the environment so that growth and poverty reduction can be lasting and benefit tomorrow's generations as well as today's.

Stimulating the private sector so that countries can become more productive and create jobs.

Reorienting government so that the public sector can complement private sector activity and efficiently undertake essential tasks such as human resource development, environmental protection, provision of safety nets, and legal and regulatory frameworks.

To bring this statement into line with World Bank policies, an additional doctrine expounded elsewhere in the same document is needed: 'No country has reduced poverty without sustained economic growth – especially growth that makes widespread and efficient use of both the poor's major asset: their labor. Growth requires increased investment, both domestic and foreign.'[24]

Given this perception, it is reasonable that increase of foreign trade and investment together with liberating internal market forces is the primary aim of Bank policy, including its SAPs. Governments further this aim by removing barriers to foreign trade and investment, increasing internal competition, creating reliable political, legal, and regulatory frameworks, developing human resources, and so protecting the environment that growth can be sustained.

Secondarily, Bank policies favor 'broad-based' growth, in which the poor participate. One senses also that the value of education, health, nutrition, and family planning is not only instrumental to broad-based economic growth. They are understood to benefit people directly as well as through supporting economic growth.

Nevertheless, from an Earthist perspective, the economistic cycle appears more dominant over the epicycles in this book than in Summers' speech. The whole vision seems skewed. First, although Bank statistics do show that on the whole increased national income leads to reduction in the number of people who earn less than a dollar a day, they do not show that the lot of the poor is regularly improved proportionally to the increase of national income. There are many countries which have grown in economistic terms with little or no benefit to the poor. In addition, Bank statistics do not take adequate account of the fact that as a country industrializes and urbanizes, the dollar-a-day figure for calculating poverty becomes seriously misleading. The quality of life sustainable in a rural village for that amount requires more in an urban context. This is obvious if we think of a First World city, but it is true already in the slums surrounding Third Word cities to which many peasants move when forced off their land by development. Bank statisticians are aware of the difficulty of making comparisons between countries and across time,[25] but leaders often quote figures misleadingly and base claims to success and directives for future policies on these misleading formulations.

Second, too little attention is paid to those countries and regions that have done much to meet the basic human needs of their people with little overall economic growth. Some of these countries have had Communist governments which have used unacceptable authoritarian means to attain these goals. But there are others that have done so in a context of personal freedom. Sri Lanka and Kerala have been mentioned above.

Unlike the examples held up by the Bank as successful instances of structural adjustment, these successes were attained in a global context that was hostile to their bottom-up approach and hence with little external assistance. They are far from perfect. But from an Earthist point of view, those concerned with development should be studying these examples and working out models that have wider applicability based upon them. It is possible that by the Bank's measure they did not reduce 'poverty,' very much. But they certainly reduced the accompaniments of poverty that make it so miserable: hunger, homelessness, and the death of children. The Bank's oft-repeated and sweeping judgment that only the global-growth model is relevant to dealing with the problems of the poor seems perverse.

Third, Earthists doubt that the increase in trade consistently celebrated by the Bank typically benefits most of the people. This increase is achieved by the export-led development patterns built into standard SAPs as well as progressive stages of GATT and the policies of the WTO. But what is exported by poor countries is often their raw materials, and when the monetary return goes to pay debts, this provides no new basis for future growth. The environment is impoverished without improvement in capital assets.

Fourth, Earthists would reverse the relation of economic growth and human and environmental concerns. The latter should be primary. Policies should be directed to meeting basic human needs, enhancing health, strengthening community life, and maintaining or restoring a healthy natural environment. The economy should be viewed as an instrument for attaining these ends.

In many countries this will entail considerable increase of production of needed goods and services, hence economic growth as conventionally measured. On the other hand, in many First World Countries, it would entail meeting legitimate human desires with reduced use of natural resources and sinks in such a way that per capita GDP would decline. The tendency of the global market, in contrast, is to concentrate wealth more in the hands of those who are already wealthy while increasing production overall. The view that continuing overall growth of this kind is sustainable in our finite physical context is not supported by scientific knowledge. As the capacity of the global physical system to support the human economy breaks down, it is the poor who suffer first and most.

VI. AN OPPOSITE CRITIQUE

This book focuses on the encounter of economism with Earthism and hence on the dominance of economistic thinking in the Bank. However, it should be noted that there are also strong voices complaining that the Bank has been unfaithful to the true economistic paradigm. In part this is because of its attention to social and environmental issues. In part it is due to the institutional restriction of the IBRD to dealing with governments. This has led it to support bureaucratically-managed projects rather than private ones.

James Bevard provides an extreme formulation of the criticism. 'The World Bank is helping Third World governments cripple their economies, maul the environment, and oppress their people.'[26] 'The Bank has greatly promoted the nationalization of Third World economies and increased political and bureaucratic control over the lives of the poorest of the poor.'[27] As examples he cites support of collectivization in Tanzania and Vietnam and of resettlement schemes in Indonesia and Ethiopia. He points out that the Bank's own figures show that 75 percent of its agricultural schemes, chiefly operated by governments, were failures.

Earthists share in much of this criticism. Indeed, the Bank itself has recognized that it has made mistakes. In many ways the Bank is now working with governments to reduce their role in the economy in just the way Bevard favors. But he may view such structural adjustment as simply another way in which government is involved in the lives of its citizens. Still, he seems to be criticizing primarily an earlier stage of the Bank's work rather than its current strongly pro-market stance.

Economistic thinkers want the Bank to move still farther in this neo-liberal direction. In January 1995 The Bretton Woods Committee, chaired by Paul Volcker, concluded that 'because economic resources and growth potential have come to reside largely in the private sector' the Bank Group 'must change the way it does business, emphasizing its role as a mobilizer of resources – private and public, intellectual and financial – not a lender of money to governments.'[28]

What these economistic critics call for is moving further in a direction which the Bank is already going. The combination of removing barriers to trade and supporting transnational private investment, to which the Bank has contributed substantially, has been highly successful in attracting investments by TNCs in some developing countries. According to Michael

Prowse, 'private flows have quadrupled since 1990 while offi-cial development assistance has stagnated. The single largest source of finance for developing countries is now foreign dir-ect investment by those once-reviled multinational companies. The bank's modest concessional loans to the poorest countries of about $5 bn a year are insignificant when set against total flows to developing nations of $230 bn a year.'[29]

The implication of Prowse's reflections is that the Bank should scale back drastically or even privatize its functions completely. If we assume, as much World Bank thinking has, that the alleviation of Third World poverty is chiefly a func-tion of capital flows to developing countries, then this task is being fulfilled far better by private corporations than by the Bank.

Prowse is not criticizing the Bank's record. Far from it! He is celebrating its success in having contributed to the global market through which growth can occur everywhere. From his point of view, the Bank has completed its mission. This mission was to create a world in which private enterprise could make its full contribution to economic growth by invest-ing everywhere. Through structural adjustment, combined with the work of GATT, this has been accomplished. The goal of a pure economism has been largely attained. For this reason the institutions that have brought this about are no longer im-portant.

NOTES

1. Lawrence H. Summers, 'The United States and the World Bank,' Remarks before the Overseas Development Council, 11 Oct. 1994, *Treasury News*, p. 4.
2. Ibid.
3. Ibid., pp. 6–7.
4. *Neighbors*, Summer 1996, p. 4.
5. Ibid.
6. Summers, op. cit., p. 4.
7. Muhammad Yunus, 'Preface: Redefining Development,' in Kevin Danaher, ed., *50 Years Is Enough: The Case Against the World Bank and the International Monetary Fund*. Boston: South End Press, 1994, p. ix.
8. Summers, op. cit., p. 7.

9.   Julie Stewart, et al., *A People Dammed: The Impact of the World Bank Chixoy Hydroelectric Project in Guatemala*. Washington: Witness for Peace, 1995, p. 31.

10. Ibid., p. 29.

11. Ibid.

12. See the moderately worded report on this incident in *The Inspection Panel Report, August 1, 1994 to July 31, 1996*. Washington: World Bank, n.d., pp. 14–17.

13. Summers, op. cit., p. 3.

14. Ibid., p. 3.

15. See William M. Alexander, 'A Sustainable Development Process: Kerala,' *International Journal of Sustainable Development*, May 1992, pp. 52–8.

16. Clifford Cobb, et al., 'If the Economy Is Up, Why Is America Down', *The Atlantic Monthly*, Oct. 1995, pp. 59–78. For more detail see Clifford Cobb, Ted Halstead, and Jonathan Rowe, *The Genuine Progress Indicator: Summary of data and methodology*. San Francisco: Redefining Progress, Sept. 1995.

17. Robert D. Kaplan, 'The Coming Anarchy: How scarcity, crime, overpopulation, tribalism, and disease are rapidly destroying the social fabric of our planet,' *The Atlantic Monthly*, Feb. 1994, pp. 44–76. Kaplan details his evidence in *The Ends of the Earth: A Journey at the Dawn of the 21st Century*. New York: Random House, 1996.

18. 'Summers on sustainable growth,' *The Economist*, 30 May 1992, p. 65.

19. Ibid., p. 6.

20. M. Bruno, 'Statement' to Multinational Group of Parliamentarians in Oversight of the IMF and World Bank, US House of Representatives Subcommittee on International Development, 21 Nov. 1994, p. 3.

21. Ibid., pp. 3–4.

22. Ibid., p. 4.

23. The World Bank, *Learning from the Past: Embracing the Future*. Washington: World Bank, 1994, p. 6.

24. Ibid., p. 18.

25. World Bank, *World Development Indicators 1997*. Washington: World Bank, 1997, pp. 50–1.

26. James Bevard, 'The World Bank and the Impoverishment of Nations,' in D. Bandow and I. Vasquez, eds, *Perpetuating Poverty*. Washington: Cato Institute, 1994, p. 59.

27. Ibid.

28. Quoted in Catherine Caufield, *Masters of Illusion: The World Bank and the Poverty of Nations*. New York: Henry Holt & Co., 1996, p. 306.

29. Michael Prowse, 'Wolfensohn's Task,' *Financial Times* (UK), 22 April 1996.

9 Can the Bank Change?

I. THE GROWTH OF THE EPICYCLES

Since 1991, one division of the Bank has been devoted to 'sustainable development.' This division does not plan or approve projects, but it does engage in research. Since in principle the Bank wants all of the development it promotes to be sustainable, the results of this research should affect all the practice of the Bank. Within this division, fresh work is being done on a paradigm that is far superior to those discussed in Chapter 8 – a paradigm of genuinely sustainable development. In this paradigm social and environmental considerations cease to be mere epicycles and play a much larger role.

Ismail Serageldin, as Vice-president for Sustainable Development, is a leader in these formulations. He points out that the Bank has defined sustainable development in a triangular way, with the corners representing economic, environmental, and social concerns.

> A proposal has to be economically and financially sustainable in terms of growth, capital maintenance, and efficient use of resources and investments. But it also has to be ecologically sustainable, and here we mean ecosystem integrity, carrying capacity, and conservation of natural resources, including biodiversity. Ecological sustainability is the domain of the biologist and the physical scientist. The units of measurement are different, the constructs are different, and the context and time scale is different. However, equally important is the social side, and here we mean equity, social mobility, social cohesion, participation, empowerment, cultural identity, and institutional development. The social dimension is the domain of the sociologist, the anthropologist, and the political scientist.[1]

Serageldin recognizes that the Bank's staff, reputation, and outlook are primarily in the economic area. Accordingly, it is important for him to acknowledge that even when economists accept the triangle, as Summers and Bruno have done, they see it differently. The economist tends to 'reduce the

economic objective to growth and efficiency, the ecological objective to natural resource management, and the social objective
to reduction of poverty.'[2] This results in the economistic circle
with epicycles discussed above. When ecologists and social scientists are given an equal role with economists in evaluating
project proposals, this model will be broken.

This would move a long way toward the Earthist model, but
it would not quite get there. In the Earthist model, economic
growth as measured by standard economics is not an autonomous goal to be given equal place with social and ecological
considerations. What is now called growth, that at which economistic policies aim, is sometimes beneficial, sometimes not.
In any case, there are physical limits to its continuance. The
goal of economic activity should be betterment of the condition of the Earth, including its inhabitants, not increased production and consumption as such.

A further important step toward an Earthist paradigm
would take place if the economist's measurement of growth
itself took account of natural and social capital. Under Serageldin's leadership important work has been carried out in
this direction as well. Some of the economists in this division,
especially Salah El Serafy, have developed new measures that
take account of environmental costs in evaluating projects.
Indeed, some have gone beyond that to propose still greater
changes in the way projects should be evaluated.

Based on their work, Serageldin, proposes shifting from
measures of income to measures of wealth, and these measures have been developed in some detail and applied to many
countries. A country's wealth includes not only its artificial
capital but also its natural capital, human resources, and social
capital. For Serageldin, sustainable growth means leaving
'future generations as many opportunities as, if not more than,
we have had ourselves.'[3]

Economic policies that aim at increasing wealth measured
in this way would differ from those aiming only at increasing
market activity. Serageldin shows in detail how market activity
can be accompanied by decline in natural, human, or social
capital. He does not imply that sustainable development can
avoid depleting some forms of capital while it increases others,
but the depletion of one form can be justified only if the
increase of another is greater.[4]

One measure developed by the Sustainable Development division is of 'genuine savings.' This is intended to replace gross savings as reported in typical national accounts as a measure of economic progress. Gross savings is the amount of the GNP that is not consumed, in other words, the amount that is invested in buildings or other lasting forms of capital, adjusted for foreign lending or borrowing. To get net savings, one subtracts depreciation of physical capital. Genuine savings are calculated by subtracting from net savings the cost of pollution and the depletion of natural resources.[5]

The resulting figure is quite different from gross savings. In Sub-Saharan Africa, North Africa, and the Middle East genuine savings have been consistently negative since 1980. On the other hand, when expenditures on education are added as contributing to social capital, the results are improved, although Sub-Saharan Africa remains slightly negative.[6]

Evaluating projects and policies by their contribution to genuine savings is far more relevant to sustainable development than using GDP figures as in the present practice. Clearly the results would move in an Earthist direction. Yet they would still fall short. For Earthists, the quality of community life, including the ability of the community to make decisions about its own future, is of central importance. Even 'genuine savings' are calculated on an individualistic basis; they can rise while community life declines.

Some indirect indications of the quality of community life can be statistically developed. The increase or decrease of crime, juvenile delinquency, addiction, family breakdown, and psychological problems are subject to partial quantification. Thus far these indicators of social improvement or decline are not included in World Bank statistics even when social factors are featured. Actually, their increase typically leads to additions to the GDP rather than subtractions.

II. GREENING THE BANK

Given, nevertheless, this great advance toward Earthist measures of progress and regress, the most important question is not that of the remaining imperfections but of the role these new indicators will play in Bank lending policies. At present, they remain 'academic' in the sense that they have their place only in the research areas. But there are indications that the new paradigm can be 'mainstreamed,' – or, as Andrew Steer, Director of the Environment Department, says 'upstreamed,' – so as 'to factor environmental concerns into the formulation of countries' sectoral strategies.'[7] Steer sees the process of introducing environmental considerations into the heart of the Bank's decision-making process as the next step in a natural progression. He writes:

> In a sense, the Bank is now entering its 'third generation' of environmental reforms. The first, in the 1987–92 period, was characterized by a major focus on reducing potential harm from Bank-financed projects and, specifically, the codification of environmental assessment (EA) procedures. The second might be termed the 'post-Rio boom.' It was characterized by a great expansion in the Bank's environmental capacity, and an aggressive effort to respond to the exploding demand for Bank assistance in environmental management.
>
> The third generation is now under way. It is characterized by three main thrusts. The first is an overriding emphasis on on-the-ground implementation. The second is a major effort to move 'upstream' from project-specific concerns in order to incorporate the environment into sectoral and national strategies. The third, undergirding all our activities, is a stronger focus on people and on social structures to find solutions and make development sustainable.'[8]

No one doubts that changing the way plans are made and projects are evaluated would involve a major transformation of the Bank's culture. The Bank continues to be dominated by economists most of whom normally think in predominantly economistic ways, or in terms of an economistic cycle with epicycles. Yet there are signs of change.

Even without abandoning the epicyclic paradigm, Summers called for assessing depreciation of resources in the process of economic planning. He recognized that in the past, where there were tradeoffs between economic growth and the environment, these had too often been made against the environment. And he commented, 'By some estimates, the bank now loans 20 times as much for the production of energy, as it does for conservation. Let me be clear: that just seems wrong.'[9]

Were Summers' 1994 position to be adopted by the Bank, it would be open to the new proposals of the Sustainable Development Division. That economists in the World Bank may really become open to using new measures can be hoped more plausibly since there has been a break in the ranks of the wider community of economists. A group of economists (including Kenneth Arrow) and ecologists meeting near Stockholm produced a joint statement. This recognized that the long-held consensus of economists that economic growth is the solution to environmental problems applied only to certain types of pollution and that issues of carrying capacity and ecosystem resilience must be taken into account as independent concerns.[10]

Still more recently, more than 2,500 economists, including eight Nobel laureates have signed a statement asserting that they 'believe that global climate change carries with it significant environmental, economic, social, and geopolitical risks, and that preventive steps are justified.' This does not lead them to give up the goal of growth, but they do affirm the desirability of reducing greenhouse emissions. Their commitment to market mechanisms leads them to conclude that the 'United States and other nations can most efficiently implement their climate policies through market mechanisms, such as carbon taxes or the auction of emissions permits.'[11]

Whether 'greening' of the Bank can occur depends on its leadership. The previous chapter pointed out that Preston and his chief economist, Bruno, had not moved as far from the pure economistic paradigm as had Summers. Without enouragement from the top, real change in the ethos of the Bank is unlikely.

Yet even during Preston's administration there was sufficient ferment within the Bank to cause astute observers to see that its established paradigm was in trouble. The environmentalist concerns that had developed under Barber and Preston led George C. Lodge of the Harvard Business School to assert that already 'in 1991, the World Bank confronted what some perceived as a crisis of purpose.'[12] Whereas the Bank continued its single-minded pursuit of growth, the critics had shown that this was damaging both to the environment and to the poor, and they were proposing a very different purpose.

Lodge quotes Richard Webb as saying that the environmentalists' challenge was 'going to turn the Bank into a real swamp. It's a major threat to what the Bank has been, because it involves a new kind of people – religious people, who have no particular respect for traditional forms of quantification and who insist on looking at the long run. They are people who are prepared to place much greater weight on uncertainties than has been the case. So there will be lots of noise, lots of delays.'[13]

Given that in 1992 the environmentalist critics constituted a tiny minority in the Bank, it is somewhat surprising that Lodge and Webb already then took their challenge so seriously.[14] In part this was due to responses that the Bank had already made. In October 1991 it had adopted an amendment to an Operational Directive (4.01) 'requiring environmental assessments of all lending operations. "The purpose of EA," the directive stated, "is to ensure that the development options under consideration are environmentally sound and sustainable..."'[15] If this were taken literally, it would transform the nature of the Bank's loans. At the very least, it provided environmentalists within the Bank with an opportunity for significant input.

III. THE NEW PRESIDENT

Wolfensohn became president of the Bank early in 1995. He has brought moral passion and deep commitment to the job. He has shown real willingness to listen to leaders of NGOs, and real desire to reform the Bank in light of many of their criticisms.

He appeared shocked at the failure of the Bank to involve the people most affected by its projects in decisions about them. He is committed to what he calls a new policy, writing in his Foreword to *The World Bank Participation Sourcebook*: 'This book presents the new direction the World Bank is taking in its support of participation, by recognizing that there is a diversity of stakeholders for every activity we undertake, and that those people affected by development interventions must be included in the decision-making process.'[16]

Wolfensohn is committed to the principle that employees be professionally rewarded according to the success of their projects rather than the amount of money they lend. His predecessor had initiated efforts to emphasize results, and Wolfensohn is carrying these forward vigorously. If he is able to effect this change, this would end the distorting incentive system built into the Bank by McNamara. The consequences of the change would probably be greater than Wolfensohn recognizes and would go far to achieve the downsizing for which the Fifty Years is Enough campaign called. This could eventually lead out of the morass of ever-increasing indebtedness of Third World nations, which is the inevitable accompaniment of the Bank's growth.

Wolfensohn is establishing a track record in other respects. During his first week in office he moved toward cancellation of Arun III in Nepal, citing the concern of the Inspection Panel that had been rejected during the previous administration. He called for a study of the Bank's experience with large dams by the Operations Evaluation Department (OED) as preliminary to a more broad based evaluation. When the OED report was criticized by NGOs as glossing over problems, the Bank moved quickly, in collaboration with the International Union for the Conservation of Nature, to call a meeting in Gland, Switzerland, April 1997, of dam-builders, NGO critics, and financiers.

The meeting was a remarkable success. 'Given more than two decades of increasingly acrimonious exchanges about the development effectiveness of large dams, most participants were not optimistic about the outcome. But by the time they left Gland, all had been surprised and excited by the breadth of the consensus on how to move forward and the issues to be addressed. Most notably, agreement was reached on the next step: A World Commission should be established to assess experience with large dams and to propose if and how they can contribute to sustainable development.'[17]

Under Wolfensohn the Bank is making its first serious effort to establish structures through which the people to be affected by a project can have real participation in its planning. This venture was planned at a meeting in Columbia in which some NGOs participated. The Bank will place NGO and Social Analysis Specialists in ten banks in Latin America and the Caribbean. They are charged with 'establishing and maintaining effective relations with NGOs in the respective country... to facilitate and strengthen public consultation and participation in Bank-assisted activities.'[18]

There have been real moves in the Bank to the bottom-up forms of development favored by Earthists. The Grameen Bank in Bangladesh has long been touted for its lending, especially to poor women, of the very small sums necessary to enable them to establish tiny businesses. This is an approach that an institution of the size and ethos of the Bank could not undertake, even if it wished. Recognizing both the excellence of the approach and the inability of the Bank itself to duplicate this elsewhere, using a grant from its net income, 'the Bank supported the successful Grameen Bank of Bangladesh in assisting other countries in replicating or expanding similar programs of making small-scale loans, primarily to poor women.'[19] It now has a small grants facility, and it is creating a micro-enterprise facility as well.

The Bank is promoting the use in some African countries of more efficient charcoal stoves. Along with this, it is working with villages whose woodlots are used to make the charcoal to insure that they sell rights to cut their trees only in a sustainable way and are paid appropriately. This program at once aids the user of the stove and the villages that supply the wood, slows the destruction of remaining forests, and reduces the release of carbon into the atmosphere.

Observers of the Bank fear that its growing enlightenment may have diminishing effect. John DeMott summarizes one plausible scenario. 'So what awaits the World Bank and Wolfensohn in the next century. First and foremost, a shifting emphasis from a world dominated by statism and government to one run more by market forces. Henry Owen, a senior consultant to Solomon Brothers, wrote in the journal *Foreign Affairs*, "Although the nature of the... services needed will vary from country to county, the changes transforming many of these countries have this in common: they will greatly enhance the roles of private sectors and reduce the roles of governments. The relative size of the operations of the World Bank, which can only deal with governments, and the

International Finance Corporation, which can only deal with private entities, may thus eventually be reversed in the most rapidly growing countries."'[20] In this case, even a shift in paradigm on the part of the IBRD would have little effect on the global scene.

If there is a shift in influence from IBRD and IDA to those branches of the Bank working with private corporations, the question of whether the social and environmental standards of the Bank apply to them as well is critical. This question came to a head over the Bio-Bio Dam in Chile with the financing of which the IFC had assisted. Some of those negatively affected by this dam appealed to the Bank's Inspection Panel, pointing out that construction of the dam did not conform to Bank standards. It was determined that the Inspection Panel did not have jurisdiction. The implication seemed to be that Bank standards did not apply to IFC projects.

However, Wolfensohn acted decisively. He appointed a high level independent commission to investigate. The results were critical of the IFC. In this case the Chilean builders repaid the IFC so as to avoid any further interference with their work. But Wolfensohn has made it clear that Bank standards will apply in future. Given minor adjustments due to the difference between governments and private business, the same policies will apply throughout the Bank family.

IV. DEBT AND STRUCTURAL ADJUSTMENT

Encouraging as all of these developments are, they do not touch two of the most important issues: debt and the SAPs. Even here there have been remarkable breakthroughs.

In his first address (1995) to the Board of Governors of the Bank Wolfensohn listed 'addressing the debt problems of the poorest countries' as second among six 'immediate priorities.'[21] In August of 1995 a World Bank paper was leaked to the press recognizing that 'a number of low-income countries had a serious, unsustainable debt problem. The paper called for a concerted and comprehensive approach to deal with the debts of the poorest countries.'[22] In April key leaders in the Bank agreed to such a plan in principle.

Nevertheless, if this was Wolfensohn's intention, he did not carry the day. At the Spring, 1996, meeting of the Bank and IMF, the Bank did not stand by the proposal, and the IMF substituted one that would have further aggrandized itself and gained nothing for poor nations. Fortunately, no decision was reached.

Some NGOs worked vigorously and successfully with allies in the BWI to keep the issue of debt relief alive. In late September these institutions instituted a new program for heavily indebted poor countries. 'The World Bank has earmarked $500 million for the first year of the initiative and up to $2 billion for an unspecified time period after that. The IMF will contribute through its existing loan structure.'[23] Poor countries will apply for help and show that they are taking suitable actions to help themselves.

Although this falls far short of the platform of the NGO campaign, it is an important breakthrough. The extent of involvement by NGOs in the process of working out the plan is also refreshing. Perhaps a new balance of cooperation and of confrontation is taking shape.

Equally hopeful, with perhaps still larger possibilities for change, is Wolfensohn's agreement to conduct a fresh study of SAPs. This might not mean much if it were to be another internal study by the Bank staff. But the study is to be jointly designed with severely critical NGOs and will be on the ground in the countries studied.

The Structural Adjustment Participatory Review Initiative represents a commitment by Wolfensohn 'to open his institution's adjustment operations to examination and critique by local civil society in order to improve the quality and local relevance of the Bank's policy-based lending.'[24] Wolfensohn has acknowledged the increase of poverty and the income gap to which the SAPs have contributed in some countries, and he is particularly seeking ways to 'promote measures which narrow income differentials.'[25]

The goal is to conduct studies in ten countries on four continents. The results are then to be presented at a forum in Washington 'where recommended changes in Bank programming will be discussed with Bank senior management and policymakers and follow-up activities planned. This forum, like the in-country ones, will be public and fully transparent.'[26]

It is too early to celebrate the outcome of this venture. It has not been easy to find ten governments willing to have their countries studied in this way. The perceptions of the Bank and of the NGOs are so different that it is difficult to agree on the questions to be asked and the criteria for evaluation. But it is not too early to celebrate the new willingness of the Bank to subject its work to public examination.

Wolfensohn professes willingness to learn, and there is no reason not to take him at his word. Not long after becoming president, he said that 'our experience has shown...that there is no simple formula for applying resources in a way that brings sustainable improvement to the lives of the 1.3 billion people in the world today who live in absolute poverty. We constantly need to question the assumptions and intellectual models that drive our thinking about how best to reach the poor, and to hear from researchers in the field about how we are doing.'[27]

Even apart from the results of this study, according to Sheldon Annis, the Bank is showing a 'new willingness to challenge policies that contribute to poverty.'[28] He identifies three ways the Bank can understand its role. 'One idea is to stabilize the financial environment for commercial banks and hope for massive new private investment. Another is to punish governments that pursue economic or political policies that the US government does not like. And another is to focus investment so that it builds upon the productive capacities of the poor majority – to stimulate economic growth from the ground up.'[29] Bank rhetoric, especially that of Wolfensohn suggests that this third way has a chance of adoption, and Annis argues that the lessons learned from the McNamara years can be combined with the new policy-based loans to implement this understanding of the Bank's role.

The Bank has learned the need 'for greater attention to the human inputs, for slower pace and scale in project implementation, for labor- rather than capital-intensive construction techniques, for more village-level procurement and contracting, and for far greater emphasis on institution-building at the grass-roots levels.'[30]

Annis believes that the social conditions in Latin America and East Asia are more favorable to such efforts now than they were in the 1960s. The poor are now better organized. Since development projects for the poor do not prove sustainable unless they mesh with complementary grassroots organizations, the Bank should 'use its influence with governments to create public frameworks under which non-governmental organizations thrive and prosper.'[31]

Annis does not directly criticize the basic principles of SAPs as described in Chapter 6. The added policies designed to benefit the poor could be viewed as epicycles on the basic model. Still, in his formulation they are more than that. He calls on the Bank to refocus 'its energies upon financing growth that builds directly upon the needs, capacities, and productivity of those who have been and are still being bypassed.'[32] If the Bank does so, and there is little in his proposal in conflict with much that the Bank is already doing, the structural adjustment it promotes would move a considerable way in the direction of the Earthist model of people-centered development.

V. WOLFENSOHN'S PARADIGM

There is every indication that Wolfensohn is providing the kind of leadership under which wider participation of affected people and social and environmental concerns can be mainstreamed. The Bank may adopt new measures of effectiveness worked out by the Sustainable Development Division. Growth as measured by GDP may truly be evaluated in terms of its contribution to broader social and environmental gains rather than viewed as the most adequate measure of progress. The Bank may devote more efforts to bottom-up development projects. It may enter into large infrastructure projects, especially dams, more rarely and with high social and environmental standards. It may expand debt forgiveness to the poorest countries. It may put still greater emphasis on consequences to the poor, and especially to poor women, in its SAPs. From an Earthist perspective, all this is to be celebrated.

The question is whether all this is to be understood in terms of expanded epicycles or a genuinely new paradigm that moves in the Earthist direction. Here, too, there are promising signs. Wolfensohn speaks of 'the need for a broader, more integrated approach to development – a new paradigm, if you will.'[33] The fuller articulation of what is needed is encouraging:

> The lesson is clear: for economic advance, you need social advance – and without social development, economic development cannot take root. For the Bank, this means that we need to make sure that the programs and projects we support have adequate social foundations:
>
> - By designing more participatory country strategies and programs – reflecting discussions not only with governments but also with community groups, NGOs, and private businesses
> - By putting more emphasis on social, cultural, and institutional issues, and their interplay with economic issues, in our project and analytical work
> - By learning more about how the changing dynamics between public institutions, markets, and civil society affect social and economic development.[34]

In this formulation, Wolfensohn seems to be making economic growth the goal and community development a means to that goal. However, elsewhere he makes clear that this is not his view.

He has said: 'Effective development . . . is not something that can be defined in terms of single projects or by increase in GDP per capita. If development were just monetary and material, candidly, after my trip to Africa, I would have been deeply depressed.'[35] Also: 'We are engaged in a process at the Bank of measuring ourselves not by dollar value, but by the impact and effectiveness of our programs in the countries in which we are operating. And we are judging that impact and effectiveness not just in economic terms, but in terms that relate to the development of each society. I hope you will see a transition of the Bank's emphasis toward a balance between financial objectives and environmental objectives, with high moral and ethical standards guiding our various endeavors.'[36]

From statements of this sort, and they are common in his writings, one could expound an Earthist paradigm for development. This would focus on the whole life of communities seeking to strengthen them socially, culturally, environmentally, and economically. The economic assistance would support the social and cultural improvement by empowering communities to take control of their own economies and direct them to socially, culturally, and environmentally desired ends. These communities would become more self-reliant and less dependent on global economic development controlled in distant centers.

The increase of production needed to meet the real needs of the poor in these communities would not require an equal or greater increase in consumption in affluent countries as does the global market. On the contrary, consumption in affluent countries should be held constant or reduced. Hence a quadrupling of consumption on the part of the poor would not put impossible strains on the capacity of the planet to supply resources and cope with pollution as would such quadrupling of total global production.

Unfortunately, there is no indication that Wolfensohn draws such conclusions from his new development paradigm. Nowhere does he speak of the need for local communities to become self-reliant or have control of their own economies. On the contrary, he seems as committed as his predecessors to the further globalization of the market with all the destruction of local community self-determination entailed. This means that a quadrupling of the consumption of the poor would have to be accompanied by a probably impossible quadrupling of consumption by the rich as well!

In its campaign to secure funding for IDA, whose mission it is to help the poorest countries, the Bank took out an advertisement stating: 'Using a mix of policy advice and finance the Bank assists [Third World] countries to create a friendly environment for the private sector and a less encompassing role for government... [and] adopt outward looking economic policies and open trade regimes.'[37] Poor countries are to be helped by helping TNCs to profit through investments in them.

Wolfensohn celebrates the great increase in MIGA's guaranteeing of private investments and in the leveraging of such investments by IFC. There is little doubt that for him, as for his predecessors, beginning with Clausen, the main engine of development will be the free global market. The new role of the Bank is to make its client states attractive for TNC investment.

Wolfensohn's paradigm, nevertheless, is not one of a cycle with epicycles. The epicycles are merging into a single vision of a healthy society in which the economy plays a contributory role. This becomes a cycle of its own with many Earthist characteristics. But it does not replace the economistic one. Working with the WTO to complete the process of globalizing the market so that TNC investments can bring prosperity to all remains an autonomous vision untouched by the growing Earthist one.

Apparently Wolfensohn sees no tension between these two cycles. It may be that in his eyes the health and strength of local communities and institutions is unaffected by loss of influence over their own economic life. Presumably he shares the belief that the rich must become richer and consume more so that the poor can have enough to subsist. Apparently he does not take seriously any limits of the capacity of the Earth to provide for human consumption. With these assumptions one can undertake to solve the problem of global poverty with a system that enhances the power and profits of great corporations far more directly than it benefits the poor.

Also, one need not attend to the impact of agribusiness and industrialization on the quality of community life, especially since the measures used to evaluate success ignore the consequences of the decay of communities. Presumably Wolfensohn believes, along with so many in the Bank, that without economic growth measured in traditional ways the other goods to which he is so committed cannot be achieved.

This is not to minimize the advance that Wolfensohn's two-cycle paradigm offers, especially as it has worked out in practice. It is to raise the question of whether the growing concern for what happens to real people and a real Earth in distinction from statistics, and the willingness to look at these matters empirically rather than through ideological glasses could lead to another step toward an Earthist paradigm. Is it possible that the Bank's president could adopt a paradigm that genuinely subordinated the goal of global economic growth, entailing the ever increasing subordination of local economies to distant actors, to the goal of the well-being of real communities of real people living in relationship to their actual physical environment and exercising some control over their lives?

Another encouraging development is that, while the econ-omistic cycle has remained, it has also changed in one sig-nificant way. The long dominant neo-liberal dogma of the autonomy of the market from the state has been opened to historical examination. The contrast between the Wolfensohn era and the preceding one on this topic is marked.

The commitment of Preston to standard neo-liberal econom-istic thinking was apparent in his dealings with Japan. Econ-omistic thinkers typically believe that markets grow best when free of bureaucratic influence. In celebrating the superiority of capitalist over Communist roads to development, neverthe-less, they have often pointed to Japan and other East Asian countries as proof. Ironically, they have ignored the actual role of government in these histories of rapid economic growth.

Critics, including the Japanese government, have noted that in most of these countries, governments played roles that are discouraged by the standard IMF and World Bank SAPs. In October, 1991, Yasushi Mieno, addressing the Bank, stated: 'Experience in Asia has shown that although development strategies require a healthy respect for market mechanisms, the role of government cannot be forgotten.'[38] Reluctantly, at Japan's insistence and expense, the Bank studied this differ-ent model of development, and still more reluctantly, at Japan's insistence, turned its internal study into a book, *The East Asian Miracle: Economic Growth and Public Policy*. This shows that 'contrary to the conventional wisdom prevailing in the English-speaking countries, it is possible to successfully man-age economies. Japan and its Asian emulators . . . have not only out-performed the centrally-planned economies, but have also done better than most of the laissez-faire economies.'[39]

In his 'Foreword' to the summary of the report, Preston recognizes that it shows that 'in some economies, mainly those in Northeast Asia, some selective interventions contrib-uted to growth.'[40] But he continued: 'The market-oriented aspects of East Asia's policies can be recommended with few reservations, but the more institutionally demanding aspects, such as contest-based interventions, have not been success-fully used in other settings.'[41] Clearly Preston was not dis-posed to favor significant changes in SAPs as a result of this study!

Wolfensohn, on the other hand, is open to learning from the successes of countries in which governments played a much larger role than called for by standard neo-liberal doctrine. Indeed, the right relation between governments and markets has become a major topic for consideration in his administration. His new chief economist, Joseph E. Stiglitz, gives central attention to this topic and approaches it in a remarkably open-ended way.[42] It is also the topic of the *World Development Report 1997*. There is no movement away from economism; for the primary focus on the state still has to do with its role in the economic order. But there is serious recognition that standard neo-liberal teaching is irrelevant to many developing countries and that its application to them has been damaging.

Japan's success began with land reform instituted by MacArthur and involved extensive protection of its internal economy from external competition. Close study of this example of economistically successful development could lead to further changes in Wolfensohn's economistic cycle. These changes would reduce the tension between this cycle and the Earthist one. Perhaps they could merge into a unified model closer to the Earthist one.

VI. THE PROSPECT

These reflections show that further evolution toward an Earthist paradigm is possible. But there are many reasons for recognizing that its actual occurrence remains unlikely. Most of the Bank's employees are fully socialized into some form of the economistic faith, usually the neo-liberal one. New employees are hired chiefly from educational institutions in which that faith is more purely preserved than in the Bank itself. Adult conversions are rare, and when the faith from which one is to convert permeates one's professional activity, such conversion is even more difficult. Even if Wolfensohn himself should want to direct the Bank's country plans, its SAPs, its infrastructure loans, and its insuring of commercial ventures to broad environmental and social ends rather than to economic growth, he will find it difficult to do so.

Hope should be tempered also by recognition of how deeply certain patterns are established in the Bank. Paradigms are self-reenforcing, since they determine that to which attention is paid and how it is interpreted. Paul Nelson analyzes this in detail. One brief selection is suggestive: 'The information generally selected for consideration in policy-making in the Bank excludes many political and socio-cultural considerations that shape the realities of social and economic change in the countries of the South. Factors that fit realities defined by the myth of development, and that are susceptible to its influence and control, are treated as the only relevant considerations... When a project or national economic policy performs unsatisfactorily, staff... choose from a narrow menu of explanations, featuring weak government commitment, poor management, and inappropriate macro-economic policy.'[43] In short it is almost impossible for evidence to count against the correctness of the Bank's economistic assumptions.

Further, the policies justified by the Bank's current paradigm and culture are just those policies that its most powerful members desire. These policies have broken the back of Third World resistance to First World domination, and they serve the interests of TNCs. David Beckmann, now president of Bread for the World, who worked for the World Bank both under McNamara and subsequently points out: 'Industrial-country governments are always strong boosters of global capitalism. They consistently urge the World Bank and IMF to convince developing countries to open up to international trade and investment. While industrial-country governments and international financial institutions often waver in their commitment to opportunity for poor people, no one ever doubts their enthusiasm for the free flow of international trade and investment.'[44] Major changes in the Bank's paradigm and programs may be impossible in these circumstances.

Furthermore, there is no reason to think that the greater realism about the positive role that national governments can play in the development process leads to any questioning of the ideal of complete globalization. Stiglitz rejoices that 'financial markets around the world are rapidly integrating into a single global marketplace, and developing countries are increasingly part of this process.' He regrets that 'the overwhelming majority of developing countries, in particular the

smaller low-income economies, still need to create the conditions to attract private capital.'[45] Thus far the economistic
cycle is securely in place.

Perhaps Earthism is now where economism was in the years
between the World Wars. In those days nationalism was rising
to a self-destructive fever pitch. Nothing could stand in its
path. It brushed aside all the obvious evidence of its destructiveness and falsity.

Nationalism did not deny the importance of the economy,
and economic arguments were sometimes used against its
extreme manifestations. But overwhelmingly, nations used the
economy for their nationalist ends. Only when this resulted in
a worldwide depression and then in an orgy of mutual destruction did the dominance of nationalism end and the hitherto
subservient devotion to the economy rise to spiritual triumph.

This is not a happy analogy. It implies that there must be
social and environmental horrors far worse than any that have
yet occurred before a change can come about. Is there an
alternative?

This brings us full circle to the possibility of the evolution of
the Bank into an Earthist institution. How much better it
would be if the noblest of the current leaders of economism
could expand the object of devotion from economic growth to
the whole Earth, including all its people, and lead the world
down a path of regeneration! If the World Bank converted
itself in this way, the transition to a just, participatory, and sustainable world could be made with far less suffering. Is this
possible?

The evidence against the economistic paradigm is strong,
and it continues to apply even when the Bank adds epicycles
or even a new complete cycle. The paradigm itself is confused.
A far more coherent and promising alternative is available.
The Bank has concerned and thoughtful leadership whose
statements already point beyond the paradigm that still gov-
erns its dominant practice. Its lending is shifting from
large-scale infrastructure and agriculture projects to health,
education, conservation, community development, and support of micro-enterprises. Wolfensohn's new unified Earthist
cycle is growing in importance. The Bank speaks regularly of
'mainstreaming' such former epicycles as participation by
those affected and the environment.[46] There could be a gradual

evolution to an Earthist paradigm or even a dramatic break-through.

If so, the Bank, with its enormous resources, might lead the way in thinking through and implementing the practical meaning of the Earthist worldview. Its leadership would greatly speed and ease the necessary process of change. But those who have long since rejected economism will not wait passively for this to happen.

NOTES

1. Ismail Serageldin, *Sustainability and the Wealth of Nations: First Steps in an Ongoing Journey*, draft for discussion at the Third Annual World Bank Conference on Environmentally Sustainable Development, 30 Sept. 1995, p. 4.
2. Ibid.
3. Ibid., p. 3.
4. See World Bank, *Expanding the Measure of Wealth: Indicators of Environmentally Sustainable Development*. Washington: World Bank, 1997.
5. Ibid., p. 8.
6. Ibid., pp. 14–15.
7. Andrew Steer, 'Ten Principles of the New Environmentalism,' *Finance & Development*, Vol. 23, No. 4, Dec. 1996, p. 7.
8. Jocelyn Mason, *Mainstreaming the Environment*. Washington: World Bank, 1995, p. xiii.
9. Lawrence H. Summers, 'The United States and the World Bank,' Remarks before the Overseas Development Council, 11 Oct. 1994, *Treasury News*, p. 7.
10. Kenneth Arrow, et al., 'Economic Growth, Carrying Capacity, and the Environment,' *Science*, 28 April 1995, pp. 520–1.
11. This statement was prepared and circulated by Redefining Progress, One Kearney Street, 4th floor, San Francisco, CA 94108.
12. George C. Lodge, 'The World Bank: Mission Uncertain,' *Harvard Business School N9–792–100*, 4 May 1992, p. 1.
13. Ibid., p. 3.
14. For an insider's account of the 'small environmental resistance movement' within the Bank, see Herman E. Daly, *Beyond Growth*, Boston: Beacon Press, pp. 5–10.
15. Lodge, op. cit., p. 5.
16. World Bank staff, *The World Bank Participation Sourcebook*. Washington: World Bank, 1996, p. ix. Note that Preston had lent his support to participatory development. On 18 Nov. 1994 in a cover letter to an earlier report he wrote: 'Paying more attention to stakeholders, and

supporting borrower efforts to engage with a range of stakeholders, opens a new area of learning for many of us. I see such learning as part of a broader effort to make the Bank a better institution – one in which we do fewer things better, with a consistent concern for effectiveness and results on the ground.' (The World Bank Operations Policy Department, *The World Bank and Participation*, Sept. 1994.)

17.   Tony Dorcey, *Large Dams: Learning from the Past: Looking at the Future*, workshop proceedings, Gland Switzerland, 11–12 April 1997. Gland: IUCN and Washington: World Bank Group, 1997, p. 4.

18.   Karen Hansen-Kuhn, 'Bank Creates NGO Liaison Positions,' *Bank-Check Quarterly*, May 1996, p. 3. See also Claudia Fumo, *The World Bank's Partnership with Nongovernmental Organizations*. Washington: World Bank, 1996.

19.   L. Sherburne-Benz, *Poverty Reduction and the World Bank*. Washington: World Bank, 1996, p. viii.

20.   J. S. DeMott, 'Came the Whirlwind,' *World Business: the Global Perspective*, July/Aug. 1996, p. 29.

21.   See James D. Wolfensohn, *People and Development*, Address to the Board of Governors, Washington, DC, 1 Oct. 1996, p. 3.

22.   John Mihevc, 'IMF Gains as Debt Talks Falter,' *BankCheck Quarterly*, May 1996, p. 1.

23.   'Policy Change for World Bank,' *The Christian Century*, 6 Nov. 1996, p. 1065.

24.   'Wolfensohn Accepts NGO Challenge to Re-Examine Adjustment Operations,' *BankCheck Quarterly*, Sept. 1996, p. 3.

25.   Ibid.

26.   Ibid., p. 14.

27.   James D. Wolfensohn, 'Opening Remarks, the World Bank as a Global Information Clearinghouse,' in Michael Bruno and Boris Pleskovic, eds, *Annual World Bank Conference on Development Economics 1996*, Washington: World Bank, January 1997, p. 10.

28.   Sheldon Annis, 'The Shifting Grounds of Poverty Lending at the World Bank,' in Richard E. Feinberg, ed., *Between Two Worlds: The World Bank's Next Decade*. New Brunswick, NJ: Transaction Books, 1986, p. 106.

29.   Ibid., p. 87.

30.   Ibid., p. 93.

31.   Ibid.

32.   Ibid., p. 108.

33.   Wolfensohn, *People and Development*, op. cit., p. 11.

34.   Ibid., p. 13.

35.   James D. Wolfensohn, 'Ethics and Spiritual Values and the Promotion of Environmentally Sustainable Development,' *Earth Ethics*, Winter 1996, p. 1.

36.   Ibid.

37.   C. Caufield, *Masters of Illusion: The World Bank and the Poverty of Nations*. New York: Henry Holt, 1996, p. 315.

38.   Yasushi Mieno, 'World Bunk,' in K. Danaher, ed., *50 Years Is Enough: The Case Against the World Bank and the IMF*. Boston: South End, 1994, p. 149.

39.   Philip Sutton, 'Transformed Market-Conforming Planning,' *Ecologial Economics Bulletin,* Jan. 1997, p. 18.
40.   *Summary: The East Asian Miracle: Economic Growth and Public Policy.* Washington: World Bank, 1993, p. iv.
41.   Ibid.
42.   Joseph E. Stiglitz, 'The Role of Government in Economic Development,' keynote address to the Eighth Annual World Bank Conference on Development Economics, in Bruno and Pleskovic, eds, op. cit. pp. 11–23; and 'An Agenda for Development for the Twenty-First Century,' keynote address to the Ninth Annual Bank Conference on Development Economics, 30 April and 1 May 1997.
43.   P. J. Nelson, *The World Bank and Non-Governmental Organizations.* New York: St. Martin's, 1995, p. 145.
44.   D. Beckman, 'Reforming the World Bank: A Personal Testimony,' *The Christian Century,* 16 April 1997, p. 396.
45.   Joseph E. Stiglitz, 'Foreword,' *Summary: Private Capital Flows to Developing Countries: The Road to Financial Integration.* Washington: World Bank, 1997, p. iii.
46.   See e.g. 'The Bank has begun a process of mainstreaming participatory approaches in its lending operations and its research and analytic work.' Fumo, *The World Bank's Partnership,* op. cit., p. 1. See also Mason, *Mainstreaming the Environment,* op. cit.

10 The Theology of Earthism

I. TELLING THE STORY OF THE EARTH

Earthism remains a minor force in global affairs, but it is a growing one. Bits and pieces of its message are forcing themselves into public consciousness. More and more people are coming to grasp its integrated and holistic vision. Even while it remains a peripheral force it matters just how its teaching and vision are shaped. Although in general Earthism has less potential for destructiveness than Christianism, nationalism, and economism, it too is subject to formulations that could prove damaging. The right formulation is important.

Earthism is not simply a set of ideas but a new paradigm, a different way of being in the world, in short, a new religion. But preceding chapters have presented it chiefly over against economism in terms of development policy. There has been no full treatment of the Earthist vision as a whole.

A religious faith can be presented in terms of its beliefs about human beings, the natural world, and what is sacred. With respect to Earthism I have done some of this in earlier books: *Is It Too Late?* (1972)[1] and *The Liberation of Life*, co-authored with Charles Birch (1981).[2] But Western religions have achieved effectiveness more by their interpretations of history than by their metaphysics. Consciously, at least, people live more by stories than by philosophical doctrines. Chapters 1 and 2 included brief summaries of the accounts of history through which Christianism, nationalism, and economism have justified themselves. The effectiveness of Earthism depends in large part on the convincing power of the story it tells. Hence, telling the story well is of great importance.

Still more is at stake in the telling of Earth's story. Like all stories, it must be selective. What it selects to include and emphasize, and how it connects these elements, determine its more concrete meaning. Already, competing sects of Earthists are telling different stories. Because all are selective from the vast range of facts, the truth of one story does not preclude that others are also true. On the other hand, true stories differ in their wisdom and value.

Christians have a major stake in just how the story is told. The best story will encompass elements of all the others and shape a unity that will make it more difficult for the enemies of Earthism to play off one sect against another. It will also give the most constructive guidance as Earthists gain more ability to implement their vision.

We have noted that highly diverse stories, capable of forming their hearers in very different ways can all be reasonably accurate in the sense that the events cited correspond fairly well to what we know of the past. Thousands of stories about the past that are true in this sense can be told. Each is based on selecting a set of past events, abstracting them from the whole, and putting them together in a form that has significant meaning for the present. The question with regard to alternative stories of this type is not which one is true in the sense of corresponding to some set of facts but which one now directs our attention and concern in the most appropriate way.

Indeed, sometimes a story that functions well is, in factual terms, highly doubtful or obviously false. This is the case with most of the ancient stories embedded in traditional religions. It is also true of the social compact story of the rise of governments told by nationalists. We may call these stories 'myths,' and we may still be guided by their deeper meanings and implications. On the other hand, we may strongly dispute and reject the meanings conveyed by stories even when they are composed of factually accurate ingredients. We see the gestalt they convey as dangerously misleading.

Nevertheless, there is an advantage in a story being true. The factual errors in ancient stories such as the biblical creation myth make the appropriation of its valuable meanings more difficult. The best Earthist story for our current use will be true in the sense of corresponding to current scientific knowledge. Among the many scientifically true stories that can now be told, it will be the one that gives the best guidance for our present life and activity.

In this chapter the judgment as to which is best in this way will be informed by Christian convictions, since those characterize the author. But explicit references to Christianity will not be numerous until the end. Most of the judgments made here from a Christian point of view should overlap with judgments made from other points of view. A vision is not less Christian because it is shared with Jews, Muslims, or environmentally concerned humanists.

Some ways of telling Earth's story, such as the biblical one, set it in the context of the story of the cosmos. This cosmic story can be told in two basic ways. It can be told so as to provide a perspective that displays the fate of the Earth as a rather minor matter, given its tininess in relation to the whole. It can also be told so as to locate the Earth in the center of the cosmic drama as the place where that drama takes on dimensions that, so far as we know, are lacking elsewhere. Earthism requires the latter account.

When we turn to the story of developments on this planet we face two similar options. This time the question is the importance of the human species. Recognizing that the planet got along without human inhabitants for billions of years and that during much of that time it sustained a rich flora and fauna, a story can encourage us to view the experiment with human creatures as a minor affair whose outcome is of secondary importance. From this point of view, whatever havoc humanity inflicts on the planet, the Earth will some day recover and continue on its way without our species. A million years more or less is not of great importance.

Or the story can be told so as to heighten the sense of the importance of human beings as the culmination of this vast process, whose capacities for both creation and destruction greatly exceed those of any other species. Indeed, those who adopt the anthropic principle imply that the whole cosmic story is oriented to the emergence of human beings. In this perspective, the survival of our species appears to be of utmost importance. Although the anthropic principle may be an overstatement, an Earthist story that does not imply the importance of the human adventure will prove dangerous.

Even in the telling of the human story a similar polarity occurs. Human beings have been around for millions of years. What we have arrogantly called history began only six thousand years ago. It is a short chapter in the larger narrative. Within that chapter the history of 'isms' recounted in Chapters 1 and 2 deals with only a small portion. The modern civilization that now threatens to destroy itself is of still shorter duration. The human story can be told so as to reconcile us to this self-destruction, with the implication that those humans who survive can reestablish a sustainable life in what is left of the Earth.

On the other hand, the story can be so told as to intensify our horror that what has taken so long to develop is now threatened by our activities. This applies both to the biosystem and to civilization. Turning away from that course of action that leads to their destruction is urgent. If Earthism is to be a force for change, the story must take this form.

All of these accounts are on a scale that treats humanity as something of a unit. Closer attention to human history brings into view the vast multiplicity of societies and cultures and the complex relations among them. The story can be told so as to minimize these details and focus on the overarching theme of how human activities have become increasingly threatening to the whole. Or the story can differentiate cultures in terms of their relations to the Earth, identifying those that achieved a sustainable relationship or developed ideologies that encourage such a relation.

If the story is to guide us today, it should differentiate cultures and take them seriously in their diversity. This will involve not only describing them in terms of how they have related to the Earth but learning from them how the story is to be told.

II. EAST AND WEST

It is fortunate that at this point in history the West has become open to learning from other cultures. There is now widespread Western interest both in the East and in societies that were once dismissed as 'primitive' or 'uncivilized.' The East provides ways of understanding society that subordinate social, political, and economic functions to spiritual ones that have less tendency to arrogate power for religious institutions or promote the sort of theological fanaticism from which the West has suffered. 'Primitive' societies show us how human beings can respect the land, understanding themselves as belonging to it rather than owning it, and can support themselves from it in sustainable ways.

Encountering these religious and spiritual visions in other cultures also enables the West to recover roots of such visions within its own. Such roots can be found in both the Greek and Hebrew sources of Western civilization. They have been a subordinate element in Christianity.

With regard to the story of the Earth, the contrast between the characteristic stories of East and West is sharp. In India the universe is depicted as eternal, and as eternally much as it is now. The Indian story posits cycles of creation and destruction, but the results did not involve ultimate loss or gain.

The spiritual implication of this cosmic vision was to detach people from the sense of historical purpose. It teaches that, while there is better and worse in history, there is no possibility of sustained advance or of final culmination. The story will go on and on without any ultimate meaning. Therefore, the goal is to be found in another dimension, in the interiority of the individual life. In that dimension there is the possibility of attaining final fulfillment.

In the West the victorious story was the Biblical one. Here the creation came into being out of nothing, or out of a valueless chaos, only six thousand years ago. The focus of attention is on the changes in the human condition that have occurred since then. Although the details of the Biblical story no longer command credulity, and it is acknowledged that the process of creation took much longer, interest continues to focus on a mere six thousand years, now because that is the period of human 'history.' The emphasis is on the uniqueness of events and their linear and progressive character. The cosmic background turns out to have little importance even for most of those who fully accept modern science.

The spiritual implication of this vision is that human history is the context of meaning. Individuals understand themselves according to their locus in this history. The stories told in Chapters 1 and 2 took this Western perspective for granted. Generally, there is a sense of progress and of the importance for individuals of participation in that progress. To be a part of this forward movement of history is to live a meaningful life.

In recent times East and West have influenced one another profoundly at this spiritual level. The encounter with the West has elicited extensive historicization in the East. Marxism has been a major instrument in this respect alongside Christian missions. Millions of Asians have come to think of the attaining of freedom from imperial masters and the achievement of economic prosperity and social justice as ultimately meaningful activities. For practical purposes, they have adopted the foreshortened Western view of history.

In the meantime, many Westerners have despaired of history as a source of meaning. Much of the current interest in spirituality expresses the fact that participation in the forward movement of history no longer satisfies, partly because it is far from clear that there is any forward movement in which to participate. Turning away from history, many are drawn to the ahistorical, deeply inward and individual, spirituality of the East.

The dominant forms of spirituality in both East and West have neglected the Earth. Although the Indian story included the birth and death of worlds, this did not lead to concern for the preservation of the Earth. These cosmic changes were beyond the influence of human beings. The East did not separate human beings far from other animals, but this acknowledgment of kinship has not lead in most instances to notable cultural sensitivity to the well-being of these other animals or to the preservation of their habitat.

The Western story originated in an account of the creation of the world by God and God's recognition of its goodness. But Western readers attended more to the fact that God gave sovereignty over the Earth to human beings. This was taken to justify exploitation of the other creatures and a preoccupation with human history. The continuance of the Earth much as it is, at least until a divinely ordained end, was taken for granted.

It is interesting that the current cosmological story told by astronomy is quite different from both. It differs from the Indian story in that it emphasizes a beginning, and probably an ending, that suggests the primacy of linear, rather than cyclical, change. Its account of our universe as fifteen to twenty billion years in age involves a drastic shift from the infinities of the Indian vision. On the other hand, this time frame vastly extends that of typical Western thinking. The implications of a forty-billion-year period from beginning to end are quite different from those of a six-thousand-year period.

Both Eastern and Western stories were products of a great historical shift from focused attention on the Earth to focused attention on human salvation in separation from the Earth. Much of what is of value in both is what has survived from the earlier vision of gathering and hunting peoples. Whatever the great religious traditions may contribute to the Earthist story, they cannot be its foundation. This must be found among primal peoples.

Among such people also there is great diversity. Yet some generalizations are possible. These people knew themselves to be part of a natural system that sustained and nurtured them. They adapted themselves to that system rather than trying to adapt that system to their needs. They depended on the fecundity of the Earth and experienced that as a gift.

It is important not to romanticize these peoples. Some of them may have treated the Earth in unsustainble ways, but these inevitably died out if they did not reform in time. They did not have the technology to extract resources from the Earth in an unsustainable way over long periods of time.

Moral virtue is not the issue for us. We want cultural resources for an Earthist story, and these primal peoples offer many. Most of all, their way of living on the Earth needs to constitute a large chapter in our Earthist history. Human beings throughout most of their sojourn on Earth understood themselves to be children of the Earth, not its owners, and they lived gratefully and sustainably with other creatures.

III. FALL AND SALVATION

Viewed in this way, the Earthist story, like the traditional Christian one, tends to be about a fall. Indeed, there are remarkable similarities. The gathering and hunting society corresponds to the gathering one located, in the Bible, in the Garden of Eden. The 'fall' began when people undertook to control nature instead of simply living as a part of it. This has something to do with a kind of knowledge, and in both the Earthist story and the Christian one, the result is the domestication of plants and animals and the subsequent building of cities. From this point, however, the Earthist story diverges from the traditional Christian one as well as alternate modern ones.

The Earthist story describes the effects of this domestication on the land as well as the associated rise of patriarchy, slavery, military conquest, and authoritarian rule. The role of environmental decay in the decline of ancient cities, still so little considered in standard Western histories, comes to the fore. The connection of the migrations of ancient people to population growth, to changes in weather, and to deterioration of the environment are featured in this history. In other words, an Earthist history will be one in which the interaction of people with the remainder of nature is prominent.

The Earthist story must pay particular attention to the rise of the great religious traditions that have dominated the 'civilized' world in the past two and a half millennia. These traditions turned attention away from the Earth and focused on history or the inner life of human individuals. They did not initiate destruction of the environment; for by the time they arose in the middle of the first millennium BCE, that had long been going on. But they ensured that cultural attention would not be directed to this phenomenon. They also encouraged condescension and even contempt, on the part of members of the now dominant cultures, for those who still adjusted their lives to the requirements of nature and shaped their religious sensibilities accordingly.

New chapters of great importance in the Earthist story will deal with the development of science and technology. Science added greatly to human understanding of the mechanisms operative in the world, and technology vastly increased the ability of human beings to adapt their environment to human wants. This led to the massive changes involved in industrialization, with its intensified pressure on natural resources and on the capacity of the environment to absorb wastes. The chemical revolution and the physical one (nuclear) carried all of this still further.

Meanwhile a major focus of the Earthist story will be on the population explosion. Through most of human history in most places the human population has been relatively small. Even a small population was able to do considerable damage, but human beings did not constitute a threat to the planet as a whole.

But beginning in the nineteenth century the rate of population growth increased rapidly. To understand who and what we now are, we must give major consideration to the enormous pressure of human numbers on the land and all its resources. Earthists view the increase of human population combined with the increased average use of resources as jointly constituting the most decisive threat to the Earth, including the human species. It is because economism ignores this threat, usually minimizes the problem of population, and consistently advocates the increased production of goods, that Earthists are impelled to confront and condemn it.

From the Earthist perspective, it is easy to depict the domestication of plants and animals, the building of cities, the rise of the world religious traditions, science and technology, the industrial revolution, and the population explosion as simply successive deepenings of the fall. And this is not false. But to tell the story in this way is to suggest that salvation would be a return to the primal form of human society. There is no possibility of such return apart from decimation of the current human population. On the basis of a hunting and gathering economy, the now impoverished biosphere could support only a fraction of the population that existed before the domestication of plants and animals, and that population was tiny in comparison with the number of people who now inhabit the globe. If return to the primal condition is seen as the Earthist alternative, the vast majority of people will rightly choose to follow economistic policies, however destructive and dangerous.

Further, it is not enough to acknowledge the impossibility of return to the primal condition. The results of domestication, cities, the religious and cultural revolution of the middle of the first millennium BCE, science, technology, industrialization, and computerization are not unmitigated evils. They cannot be dismissed simply as a succession of falls. If the Earthist story is to gain wide acceptance, it must appraise these developments fairly, noting the heavy losses and their now frightening consequences, but also recognizing the cultural and economic riches they have produced. If we are to move forward in Earthist terms, we must use the positive contributions of all these developments. We will begin by considering the spiritualities of East and West whose inadequacy was acknowledged above.

The Earthist cannot support the use of Eastern spirituality to direct attention away from history. Today it is supremely important that people care what happens in the future and appraise what is happening now in light of that concern. But Eastern spirituality does have the ability to reduce our attachment to the worldly goods that economism undertakes to provide us. It is often associated with a simpler, less-consumptive style of life that is, in fact, far more satisfying than participation in the economistic struggle. It can effect these changes among contemporary urban people in terms of their most highly developed understanding and concern. It can also overcome the egotism that afflicts Earthists as much as other activists and thus improve their collective effectiveness. It can teach us much about our bodies as spiritual organisms contributory to salvation.

The Earthist cannot support the Western focus on historical salvation cut off from appreciation of the value and fragility of the Earth. But Earthism shares with much of the Western tradition a world-affirming spirit. It shares the judgment that we must appraise what we do now in light of its effect on history. It can find resources in both the Greek and the Hebrew heritage to broaden that sense of history to include the natural world. It can learn the importance of appreciating the integrity and rights of each individual as an individual at the same time that each is understood as part of a larger system. And it can learn much from the millennia-long reflections of the West on the complexities and ambiguities of history with which Earthists, too, must now wrestle.

Earthism cannot simply celebrate the rise of science, technology, and industrialization, as does economism. But it must recognize that the natural sciences provide us the knowledge both of what is going wrong with the Earth and of ways of responding. It can also rejoice that the natural sciences have themselves led the way in overcoming the mechanistic view of nature that has encouraged its ruthless exploitation and in showing the kinship of human beings with all the other species of living creatures. Although industrialization has greatly accelerated the rape of the Earth, it continually generates new techniques whose use has the potential of providing us with desirable goods in a far less unsustainable way.

Such positive appraisal of developments that have alienated human beings from the Earth and led to its abuse is important. These developments must be mined for their contributions to what is now needed for the salvation of the Earth including its human population. But it is not enough to affirm them only in this way. There are great inherent values in our religious, cultural, intellectual, artistic, and economic achievements, even when they make no contribuition to long-term survival. Earthism becomes another form of fanaticism when it measures everything by its contribution to the sustainability of the Earth.

The Earthist history focuses on human interaction with the rest of the world together with human reflection about this interaction. It recognizes that there can be great value in human artifacts that are relatively neutral with respect to the healthy survival of the Earth. But this affirmation of multiple values still does not suffice.

In our time this Earthist story is viewed with suspicion not only by adherents of economism but also by liberationists. This is because the Earthist story too often minimizes questions of justice among human beings. It implies that the way societies organize themselves internally is secondary to how they relate to the Earth.

As long as the Earthist story is told in this way, it will not succeed. It can succeed only if it serves to unify the current human victims of economistic policies with all those who care for the human future and for other creatures. It has a chance of doing this, because the Earth includes all the species and all the individuals who make it up. But the right telling of the story is not an easy matter.

This telling requires that, from the beginning, the story include the structures of power in human societies. The gathering and hunting society is to be described not only by how it adapted to its environment but also how, in some instances, it gave full respect to all its members and allowed extensive participation in decision making. It minimized the use of force internal to the tribe and conflict among tribes. That there were many exceptions to these positive achievements is not to be concealed, but that our ancient ancestors also developed models of social justice and peace correlated with adaptation to the natural world is to be affirmed. These should be celebrated and studied.

In tracing the beginnings of human disturbance of the environment through domestication of plants and animals, building cities, and industrialization, it is important to consider also what was happening to human relationships within and between societies. On the whole, these worsened. Hierarchical organization of society, patriarchy, slavery, and war, all became dominant characteristics of the societies that emerged. Yet new forms of community also contributed their riches.

The point, of course, is that the histories of the oppression of people and of the degradation of nature have been intimately interconnected. The past five hundred years of European conquest of the Western hemisphere are not an exception. Genocide against indigenous people and drastic impoverishment of the nonhuman world have been inextricably connected.

Today the economistic policies that are speeding up the exhaustion of resources in so many Third World countries are also depriving many of their people of access to the land on which they have lived. Peasants are driven from the land into slums unfit for human habitation, and even when they find work in the new factories, their wages and working conditions are miserable. Hunger increases, not because the land cannot feed people, but because it is used to produce for export rather than for local needs.

When the story is told in this way the implication is clear. There cannot be a reversal of patterns of destroying the Earth that does not involve the liberation and empowerment of oppressed people everywhere. Equally, there cannot be liberation and empowerment of oppressed people without restoration of the Earth. The Earthist story can include the liberationist one and gain the credibility and support it requires to supersede the economistic one.

IV. CHRISTIAN EARTHISM

Is Earthism the panacea? Is it the final religion? No. The Earth is not worthy of supreme devotion and loyalty, and these limits will eventually show themselves. The Earth is not God, and God is not the Earth. Should Earthlings ever encounter creatures from other parts of the universe, the idolatrous character of an unqualified Earthism would immediately become manifest. Even now devotion to the Earth may discourage adequate sensitivity to the needs of the individual creatures who jointly make it up, especially the human ones. In addition, Earthism is always in danger of taking on the all too typical Western note of fanaticism.

Yet the Earth is a far more inclusive and suitable object of devotion than Christianity, a nation, or economic growth. The policies to which this devotion gives rise are far more favorable to the well-being of all creatures. From the perspective of Christian faith in God, Earthism is a great improvement over other real options. Its rise should be greeted enthusiastically by Christians, and it should be given strong support.

At the same time Christians should take a keen interest in the way the theology of Earthism is formulated. While it struggles to overcome the hegemony of economism, theological differences seem to be secondary. Instead of arguing over different interpretations of Earthism, we need to work together. Yet even in order to work together we need to tell our story well. And should Earthists be successful, then doctrinal differences of other types will also prove important.

For example, some Earthists are basically scientific materialists in their explicit doctrines. The deep personal commitment of these Earthists is not to be questioned, but their explicit formulations do not justify their passion and commitment. Furthermore, if these are taken with full seriousness, they do not support concern for individual human beings when the human population overall is excessive. The fact that those who assert these doctrines do not usually draw from them their destructive implications does not mean that others will not. Christian Earthists should contribute to Earthist theology in ways that subsume what is true in scientific materialism in a much larger vision of reality.

Since much of the leadership of Earthism has come from scientists, and since many scientists think of themselves as materialists, this argument needs to be unpacked. The criticism of scientific materialism is not intended as criticism of the valuable leadership some who call themselves scientific materialists are giving to the Earthist cause. Nor does it imply that they personally think or act in the ways that follow logically from their metaphysics. The point is only that at some point others may draw the logical conclusions.

Consider an analogy from the age of Christianism. Millions of Christians believed that what happens to one after death is more important than what happens during this life. Many of them also believed that what happens after death followed from the beliefs one held at the point of death. A logical conclusion would be that anything one could do to make another accept the needed beliefs should be done.

In the vast majority of instances, no action or recommendation of action followed from these widely held doctrines. They were relatively harmless. But under certain circumstances they led a few to practice torture for the sake of the tortured! They led many others to acquiesce in this practice.

In the age of nationalism some believed that there was real superiority attaching to the members of their nation, or that their culture had values that would benefit others. For most nationalists most of the time such beliefs did not have major consequences. But in light of slavery, manifest destiny, the white man's burden, segregation, the Holocaust, and apartheid, we recognize now that they were far from harmless.

For scientific materialists things, including people, are nothing more than they can be known to be scientifically. Also, science is understood to know everything as material or as purely objective. Subjectivity disappears or is reducible to a by-product of the motion of objects. Also, scientific information may be understood to point to the threat to the biosystem arising from an excessive number of human beings.

Now in the vast majority of instances, no action or recommendation of action follows from these beliefs. They are relatively harmless. However, a few conclude from them that when natural forces threaten a large number of human lives, the correct response is to do nothing. These natural forces are freeing the world from surplus population. Circumstances might arise in which it would seem appropriate for human beings to take the initiative in disposing of such surpluses. Those steeped in these beliefs would have no rational reason to protest.

The problems go even deeper. Scientific materialism provides us with a world of facts from which no values whatsoever can be drawn. The previous argument assumed a bias in favor of a healthy biosphere or simply a personal bias against having to share the goods of the world with too many people. A strict scientific materialism treats any such biases, desires, hopes, or preferences as equally valid or invalid. They simply are what they are, by-products of the play of matter. There is, in principle, no basis for evaluating them. There is no *reason* then to care about the fate of the Earth or of the human species or of individual human beings.

Again, this does not in the least imply that individual scientific materialists fail to hold to values of the noblest order. It does raise the question of whether they derived these values from their scientific materialism or whether they have retained these values in spite of this materialism. So far as they are concerned as persons, this makes little difference. But when we evaluate ideas, we must ask about their effect on others who imbibe them early and take them seriously. Theoretical beliefs are important.

This chapter has considered Earthist theology primarily in terms of its story instead of its metaphysics. The proposal for telling the Earthist story above is informed at every step by Christian values and concerns. In particular the concerns to display the convergence of caring for exploited humans and for other creatures, to emphasize the value of individuals, especialy human ones, to locate ourselves in history, to learn from the great spiritualities of history, to affirm the ambiguous values of each stage in history, and to support the cause of liberation express Christian convictions. But these values are shared by many who are not Christian. And this is important. Earthism can overcome the dominance of economism only if it has the support of persons from many traditions and communities.

Nevertheless, there will be differences. For Christians the Earthist story centers finally in Jesus Christ. It is this centrality that constitutes a story as Christian. Christians can hope that others will appropriate the story in a way acceptable to Christians without this center, so that a helpful story will not be told only by Christians. But for those of us who are Christians, only the centered story is fully adequate.

We come to this centering confessionally. We ask ourselves whence arises our deep caring for the Earth and all its creatures. There may be an element of self-interest in this caring; for we enjoy the richness of this natural and human world. But our caring goes far beyond that. It is a caring for neighbors, defined simply as others, as beings who exist, just as we exist, with their own inherent value. That caring is, for us, inseparable from the perception of these beings as creatures, prized and loved by God as we are prized and loved by God.

We understand God as the creative Spirit who through the ages has called life into being in all its rich panoply, who prizes the great variety of things. This Spirit works in and through all things and can work through us for the enrichment of creation if we allow this. To destroy casually and without justification what God has brought so painstakingly and lovingly into being is a sacrilege. It inflicts a loss not only on those that are destroyed and on other creatures who now miss the lost ecosystems and the extinct species, but also on God.

Our understanding of God and the world has come to us in a community rooted and formed by the Bible. It is there that we learn of our shared creatureliness, of God's purposes, and of our role. This community came into being through the life, teaching, death, and resurrection of Jesus whom we call the Christ. Through him we have been engrafted into ancient Jewish history so that it has become our own.

This history is not an idealized one. It tells of people as they are with all their strengths and weaknesses, virtues and sins. It reminds us that the best of us are ignorant sinners. But it assures us of the possibiity of repentance and of God's welcoming joy when we do repent.

This repentance is not simply for personal sins. Israel repented at times. The church often needs to repent and sometimes does so. Today it needs to repent of its long indiffernce to the destruction of other creatures by human beings. In doing so it lives in healthy continuity with the best of its past. We are held to the Christian faith not because we suppose it provides final answers or makes our lives pure and virtuous, although it does call us to strive to serve God and fellow creatures. We are held to our faith because it offers a story sufficiently complex to illumine the changing situation in which we find ourselves and sufficiently open to assimilate what is best in other stories.

Jesus is central for us because it is through him that we have been engrafted into the story of Israel. We realize also that we read that ancient story through him and the faith he inspired. This leads us to appropriate the Hebrew scriptures in a way that is somewhat different from those Jews who do not follow

Jesus. We need not claim any superiority for our reading and telling of the story, but confessionally we recognize the centrality of Jesus for us in this respect as well. Our understanding of God is shaped by the way we encounter the divine in Jesus.

I have spoken here for *Christian* Earthists, having affirmed that persons come to the Earthist story in diverse ways. It is obvious, also, that it is possible to read history with Jesus as the center and not be an Earthist. Indeed, that is the majority position of Christians to the present day. But the situation is changing. Repentance is occurring. More and more Christians find that Jesus points us to the God who is the God of all creatures and who is served through the service of all creatures. For practical purposes this directs us to the Earth with all its inhabitants, especially the human ones, as the locus of our Christian service.

NOTES

1. John B. Cobb, Jr., *Is It Too Late?* Reprinted: Denton, TX: Environmental Ethics, 1995.
2. Charles Birch and John B. Cobb, Jr., *The Liberation of Life: From the Cell to the Community*. Reprinted: Denton, TX: Environmental Ethics, 1990.

Index

Note: abbreviations used in index subheadings are explained on p. ix.